how2become.com

Police Situational Judgement Tests

How to pass the police officer situational judgement exercises

www.How2Become.com

Attend an online Police Officer training webinar by visiting:

www.PoliceCourse.co.uk

Get more products for passing any selection process at:

www.How2Become.com

Orders: Please contact www.How2Become.com

You can order through Amazon.co.uk under ISBN 9781911259343, via the website www.How2Become.com or through Gardners.com.

ISBN: 9781911259343

First published in 2017 by How2Become Ltd.

Updated in 2020

Get more guides, books and training courses at the website www.How2Become.com.

Contents

2020 UPDATE FOR ONLINE ASSESSMENT CENTRE

Hello, and welcome to *Police Situational Judgement Tests*. In this book, we'll be teaching you all of the ins and outs of the Police Situational Judgement Test. In order to become a police officer, almost every constabulary will require you to take some form of situational judgement test.

Whilst the selection process for becoming a police officer is highly competitive, there are a number of things that you can do to increase your chances of success, and they are all contained within the guides and services we provide at How2Become.com.

The guide itself has been split up into useful sections to make it easier for you to prepare for the test. Read each section carefully and take notes as you progress. Don't ever give up on your dream; if you really want to become a police officer, then you CAN do it. The way to approach an application for a job of this nature is to embark on a programme of 'in-depth' preparation, and this guide will show you exactly how to do that.

If you need any further help with the police officer tests, application form or interview, then here at How2Become we offer a wide range of products and courses to assist you. These are all available through our online shop at **www.How2Become.com.**

The Police Core Competencies

The role of a police officer is made up of a number of core competencies. 'Core competencies' is the name for the key behavioural expectations of a police officer. By following the core competencies, police officers can ensure that they uphold the high standards of the police service, maintain public trust in the police, and offer the best possible service to citizens of the UK. You may receive these competencies in your application pack, or alternatively they can usually be found on the website of the service you are applying to join. Whatever you do, make sure you get a copy of them, and have them by your side when practising for the assessment centre.

The core competencies that form the basis of the police officer role are similar to the following. Please note that the core competencies can, and do, change from time to time so it is important to confirm that they are correct.

PUBLIC SERVICE

Demonstrates a real belief in public service, focusing on what matters to the public and will best serve their interests. Understands the expectations, changing needs and concerns of different communities, and strives to address them. Builds public confidence by talking with people in local communities to explore their viewpoints and break down barriers between them and the police. Understands the impact and benefits of policing for different communities, and identifies the best way to deliver services to them. Works in partnership with other agencies to deliver the best possible overall service to the public.

OPENNESS TO CHANGE

Positive about change, adapting rapidly to different ways of working and putting effort into making them work. Flexible and open to alternative approaches to solving problems. Finds better, more cost-effective ways to do things, making suggestions for change. Takes an innovative and creative approach to solving problems.

SERVICE DELIVERY

Understands the organisation's objectives and priorities, and how own work fits into these. Plans and organises tasks effectively, taking a structured and methodical approach to achieving outcomes. Manages multiple tasks effectively by thinking things through in advance, prioritising and managing time well. Focuses on the outcomes to be achieved, working quickly and accurately and seeking guidance when appropriate.

PROFESSIONALISM

Acts with integrity, in line with the values and ethical standards of the Police Service. Takes ownership for resolving problems, demonstrating courage and resilience in dealing with difficult and potentially volatile situations. Acts on own initiative to address issues, showing a strong work ethic and demonstrating extra effort when required. Upholds professional standards, acting honestly and ethically, and challenges unprofessional conduct or discriminatory behaviour. Asks for and acts on feedback, learning from experience and developing own professional skills and knowledge. Remains calm and professional under pressure, defusing conflict and being prepared to step forward and take control when required.

DECISION MAKING

Gathers, verifies and assesses all appropriate and available information to gain an accurate understanding of situations. Considers a range of possible options before making clear, timely, justifiable decisions. Reviews decisions in the light of new information and changing circumstances. Balances risks, costs and benefits, thinking about the wider impact of decisions. Exercises discretion and applies professional judgement, ensuring actions and decisions are proportionate and in the public interest.

WORKING WITH OTHERS

Works co-operatively with others to get things done, willingly giving help and support to colleagues. Is approachable, developing positive working relationships. Explains things well, focusing on the key points and talking to people using language they understand. Listens carefully and asks questions to clarify understanding, expressing own views positively and constructively. Persuades people by stressing the benefits of a particular approach, keeps them informed of progress and manages their expectations. Is courteous, polite and considerate, showing empathy and compassion. Deals with people as individuals and addresses their specific needs and concerns. Treats people with respect and dignity, dealing with them fairly and without prejudice regardless of their background or circumstances.

IMPORTANT 2020 UPDATE

Due to COVID-19 in the UK in 2020, the College of Policing began using a new online assessment centre. The new assessment centre comprises of 3 parts:

1. Situational Judgement Test
2. Competency-Based Interview
3. Written Exercise and Briefing Exercise

Throughout the online assessment centre, candidates are assessed against a set of new core competencies. These competencies were previously being trialled by the Metropolitan Police and a few other forces.

You may notice that the new competencies are very closely related to the old ones.

Learn about the new core competencies on page 189

How to Use These Competencies In The PSJT

As you can see, there is quite an extensive list of expectations for a police officer. The good news is, it's fairly easy to use these in the PSJT. All you need to do is look at each response, and weigh up how well it matches the competencies. For instance, if you see a response like this...

'Inform the man that the police service is no place for a religious individual'

...then you can safely assume that this would be at the very least an inefficient response, and more likely counterproductive, depending on the situation. Below we've provided you with a sample question.

Sample Police Situational Judgement Question

The following is a sample PSJT question for you to try. Following the question is a breakdown of how the answer has been reached.

Sample question

You are sitting in the staff canteen, when three other members of the constabulary sit down at your table. As you engage in friendly discussion with them, two of the members begin to mock the other person for his religion. Although they are only joking, you can see that the individual in question has been upset by these comments.

1. Join in, it's just a bit of banter.

Efficient / Fairly Efficient / Inefficient / Counterproductive

2. Speak up, and inform your colleagues that they should have more respect for other religions.

Efficient / Fairly Efficient / Inefficient / Counterproductive

3. Ask the offended colleague to speak to you in private afterwards, where you will discuss the comments.

Efficient / Fairly Efficient / Inefficient / Counterproductive

4. Try to change the subject.

Efficient / Fairly Efficient / Inefficient / Counterproductive

How to tackle the question

Whenever you are answering this type of police situational judgment question, always try to focus your answer around the core competencies of the police.

'Join in, it's just a bit of banter.'

Answer: Counterproductive

Explanation: This is a counterproductive response. Religion is not something that should be mocked, and you can clearly see that the individual in question has taken the remarks badly.

'Speak up, and inform your colleagues that they should have more respect for other religions.'

Answer: Efficient

Explanation: This is an efficient response, as you are clearly demonstrating to the affected individual that discrimination of any kind will not be tolerated, as well as admonishing your colleagues for their behaviour.

'Ask the offended colleague to speak to you in private afterwards, where you will discuss the comments.'

Answer: Fairly Efficient

Explanation: This response is fairly efficient. You are showing your colleague that discrimination is not acceptable, but at the same time you are not demonstrating this to the individuals who have upset him.

'Try to change the subject.'

Answer: Inefficient

Explanation: This is an inefficient response. You need to make sure that the problem is addressed.

Tips for passing the Situational Judgement Test

There are several things you can do in order to help improve your scores during the PSJT. The following tips will help you to prepare effectively and improve your overall ability to pass this type of psychometric test:

TIP 1 – There are many types of Situational Judgement Tests available on the market. Just because you are applying to become a police officer, doesn't mean you should focus solely on police officer related SJTs. Obtain as many SJT questions as possible, from a variety of different genres, and practise accordingly.

TIP 2 – When you read the question, you will be presented with a 'situation'. Read the situation quickly before scanning each of the presented options. Look for the safest option first, and then look for the option you would be least likely to carry out at all. Then, assess the final two options and place them in order of priority based on what you would do in that type of situation.

TIP 3 – You do not need to be a police officer in order to pass the police officer related situational judgement test questions provided within this book. What you do need to be is professionally conscious, and have a good level of common sense. When assessing the situation and presented options, always err on the side of caution. Don't take silly risks.

TIP 4 – Be entirely honest in how you answer the questions. This is very important. The role of a police officer involves a high degree of trust, integrity, professionalism, safety and a strict adherence to rules and procedures. The test is designed to assess how you would perform or react to given situations. You should also be aware that the police constabulary may ask you questions during the interview based on the answers you provide during the Situational Judgement Test. For example, if you answer a question during the PSJT that indicates you prefer to work alone as opposed to working as part of a team, yet you contradict yourself during one of the interview questions and state that you prefer to work as part of a team, this could lose you marks and imply you are dishonest. By answering the questions honestly during the test, you will not have to worry about how you answer the questions during the interview.

TIP 5 – Preparation is key! In the weeks leading up to your test, work hard to improve your skills in the testing areas. In addition to the tests contained within this guide there are numerous other testing resources available at www.how2become.com. Try out as many test questions as possible and make sure you learn from your mistakes.

TIP 6 – Get a good night's sleep before the test day and don't drink any alcohol or caffeine in the build up to the tests. It is important that you drink plenty of water in order to keep yourself hydrated.

TIP 7 – On the morning of the test, get up early and have a final run through of some sample test questions, just to get your brain working.

TIP 8 – Eat a good healthy breakfast such as bran flakes and a chopped-up banana. Don't eat anything too heavy that will make you feel bloated or sluggish – remember, you want to be at your best.

TIP 9 – Wear a smart, formal outfit for the testing day. The reason for this is some candidates will be casually dressed. However, you are applying for a professional career and therefore appearance is important. It is better to stand out for the right reasons. As a police officer you are a role model for the constabulary you are applying to join. Make the effort to dress smart.

TIP 10 – On the day of your test, check the news for any potential traffic problems and leave in good time to arrive at the test centre with plenty of time to spare. Take a small bottle of water with you to help keep you hydrated.

Now, have a go at the first practice test in this book. The first test is a police related situational judgement test, where the questions will put you in the position of an actual officer. Check your answers at the back of the book to see how you get on!

Please note: none of the following questions or scenarios relate to actual events. The questions, scenarios and provided answers are completely fictitious. These questions are designed purely to provide preparation for those taking a situational judgement test. They are not representative of real questions or scenarios, nor are any laws, statements or suggested answers based on real life facts.

You can assist your preparation by reading the police code of ethics document, located on the College of Policing website. However, as an aspiring police officer, when undertaking the police situational judgement test you will most likely not be required to understand any laws or methods of policing. You should always answer the questions truthfully.

Police Situational Judgement: Practice Test 1

Test 1 contains 50 practice questions. Answers on page 104.

Q1.

> You are policing a local shopping centre. As you are walking past a clothing shop on the top floor, a man comes running past you at full speed. He knocks into you and falls to the ground. As he falls, he drops the bag in his hand, and a t-shirt falls out. You notice that the t-shirt still has the magnetic store tag on it.
>
> **Man:** 'Sorry mate, didn't see you there! Must dash!'

1. Help the man to his feet, apologise for knocking him over, put the t-shirt back in his bag for him and wish him a good day.

Efficient / Fairly Efficient / Inefficient / Counterproductive

2. Help the man to his feet and examine the t-shirt. Place him under arrest, then conduct a stop and search for a receipt for the t-shirt and question the man on where he got it from.

Efficient / Fairly Efficient / Inefficient / Counterproductive

3. Ask the man to come with you to the security office, so that you can investigate further. Explain to him that this is a precautionary step.

Efficient / Fairly Efficient / Inefficient / Counterproductive

4. Pin the man to the floor and proceed to arrest him.

Efficient / Fairly Efficient / Inefficient / Counterproductive

Q2.

> You are taking your lunch break at police HQ. As you sit down in the canteen, one of your colleagues approaches you. He sits down at your table and proceeds to inform you that he is a homosexual, and that you are the first person he has told.
>
> **Man:** '*Please try to keep this a secret, I'm scared of how I'll be treated if other people find out.'*

1. Inform your colleague that you have the utmost respect for him, regardless of his sexual preferences, and that his secret is safe with you.

Efficient / Fairly Efficient / Inefficient / Counterproductive

2. Inform your colleague that there is no reason to be ashamed of this, and encourage him to tell other people at the station.

Efficient / Fairly Efficient / Inefficient / Counterproductive

3. Inform your colleague that there is no place for people like him in the police force, and that he should hand in his badge.

Efficient / Fairly Efficient / Inefficient / Counterproductive

4. Inform your colleague that his secret is safe with you, before changing the topic of conversation.

Efficient / Fairly Efficient / Inefficient / Counterproductive

Q3.

> **You are the senior officer at a local police HQ. One day, one of your staff members knocks on your door. After inviting her in, she tells you the following:**
>
> **Staff member:** *'I'm really sorry sir, but I've made a mistake. While sorting through my paperwork, I accidentally shredded some of the key case reports on the Michelle Anthony murder investigation.'*

1. 'It's okay, we'll just have to proceed without those documents for now. Hopefully they won't be too important.'

Efficient / Fairly Efficient / Inefficient / Counterproductive

2. 'This is a disaster. You've derailed the entire investigation. I'm afraid you're sacked.'

Efficient / Fairly Efficient / Inefficient / Counterproductive

3. 'Okay, don't panic. I'll contact the senior administrator, who should have photocopies of the forms. Later this afternoon though we'll have a serious chat about this.'

Efficient / Fairly Efficient / Inefficient / Counterproductive

4. 'Can you explain to me how this happened? This is a very serious incident.'

Efficient / Fairly Efficient / Inefficient / Counterproductive

Q4.

> You are on duty with a fellow officer, at your local shopping centre. The two of you are in the middle of patrolling the top floor, when you pass by a particular clothing shop. Your fellow officer gets very excited, dashes into the shop and starts trying on denim jackets.
>
> **Fellow officer:** *'I love this shop! I might have to buy a few things from here!'*

1. Inform your fellow officer that they are acting very unprofessionally, and tell them to get back to work.

Efficient / Fairly Efficient / Inefficient / Counterproductive

2. Leave your fellow officer to it. It's not your problem if they want to mess around.

Efficient / Fairly Efficient / Inefficient / Counterproductive

3. Inform your fellow officer that you'll be reporting them to your head of station for this.

Efficient / Fairly Efficient / Inefficient / Counterproductive

4. Laugh. They are only having a bit of fun.

Efficient / Fairly Efficient / Inefficient / Counterproductive

Q5.

You are on duty by yourself, walking through a residential area. Your partner has been taken ill, and you are due to receive a new partner shortly. As you walk through the area, you see a man on a ladder, climbing in through the upstairs window of a house. There are no cars parked on the driveway.

1. Ignore it. He's probably just forgotten his keys.

Efficient / Fairly Efficient / Inefficient / Counterproductive

2. Immediately call the station to ask for backup. You may need help to apprehend the criminal.

Efficient / Fairly Efficient / Inefficient / Counterproductive

3. Wait for the man to exit the property, and then confront him.

Efficient / Fairly Efficient / Inefficient / Counterproductive

4. Immediately attempt to enter the property yourself. You need to stop the man before he gets away.

Efficient / Fairly Efficient / Inefficient / Counterproductive

Q6.

> Overnight, the local park has been declared as a crime scene. You have been tasked with ensuring that nobody enters the park, which has been cordoned off with crime scene tape. All of a sudden, a man approaches you:
>
> **Man:** *'Hi there, I left my bag in the park yesterday afternoon. It should be on the bench near the water fountain. Is it okay if I go in and get it? I'll only be 2 minutes.'*

1. 'I'll have to ask my senior officer about that, give me a moment.'

Efficient / Fairly Efficient / Inefficient / Counterproductive

2. 'Sure, go right ahead, just tell them that I let you in.'

Efficient / Fairly Efficient / Inefficient / Counterproductive

3. 'I'm sorry sir but this is a crime scene, we can't allow anyone to enter.'

Efficient / Fairly Efficient / Inefficient / Counterproductive

4. 'Since your bag has been left at the scene, it could be used as evidence. For this reason, I'm afraid I can't retrieve it for you.'

Efficient / Fairly Efficient / Inefficient / Counterproductive

Q7.

> **You are working at police HQ. You have a mountain of paperwork to get through, when your senior officer approaches you.**
>
> **Senior Officer:** *'Hey, I need you to fill in this form urgently, it's in regard to the Conningway case. Can you get it back to me in the next hour?'*

1. 'If you say please.'

Efficient / Fairly Efficient / Inefficient / Counterproductive

2. 'I'll do my best, although I've got a lot of paperwork to complete. Would you prefer me to prioritise this form?'

Efficient / Fairly Efficient / Inefficient / Counterproductive

3. 'No chance, you'll have to wait until tomorrow.'

Efficient / Fairly Efficient / Inefficient / Counterproductive

4. 'Sure, I'll give it immediate priority.'

Efficient / Fairly Efficient / Inefficient / Counterproductive

Q8.

> You are on evening patrol with another officer. As you pass the local pub, a man staggers outside. He is bleeding from the nose. Another man follows him out and knocks him to the floor with a punch. The two begin to scuffle on the ground.
>
> **Fellow officer:** *'Oh dear. Let's call for backup, there's no point in endangering ourselves by getting involved.'*

1. Inform your fellow officer that it's your duty to protect the public, and immediately intervene.

Efficient / Fairly Efficient / Inefficient / Counterproductive

2. Allow your fellow officer to call for backup, while trying to intervene yourself.

Efficient / Fairly Efficient / Inefficient / Counterproductive

3. Agree with your fellow officer. There's no point putting yourself in danger. **Efficient / Fairly Efficient / Inefficient / Counterproductive**

4. Encourage your fellow officer to intervene, while you call for backup.

Efficient / Fairly Efficient / Inefficient / Counterproductive

Q9.

The day is Thursday. You've been working with your current partner for just under a month now, but have noticed that this person keeps clocking out from your shifts early. As you approach the end of the day, he says:

'Right, I'm off now. See you tomorrow.'

The time is 16:30, and he's due to finish at 17:00.

1. 'Alright, bye.'

Efficient / Fairly Efficient / Inefficient / Counterproductive

2. 'You've finished early a few times recently. Your shift isn't meant to end till 5pm.'

Efficient / Fairly Efficient / Inefficient / Counterproductive

3. 'I'm going to tell police HQ about this.'

Efficient / Fairly Efficient / Inefficient / Counterproductive

4. 'Our shift doesn't finish for another half an hour. Get back here, or else…'

Efficient / Fairly Efficient / Inefficient / Counterproductive

Q10.

You are on your lunchbreak, and stop by a local newsagent. As you walk through the store, you notice a young man with a bag of sweets under his arm leaving the shop. The man doesn't seem to have visited the till, but the alarm isn't going off.

1. Approach the shopkeeper and inform him that you believe someone has just stolen from his store.

Efficient / Fairly Efficient / Inefficient / Counterproductive

2. Ignore the situation. The man has probably paid.

Efficient / Fairly Efficient / Inefficient / Counterproductive

3. Follow the man out of the shop and question him.

Efficient / Fairly Efficient / Inefficient / Counterproductive

4. Ask the shopkeeper if you can take a look at the shop's CCTV footage.

Efficient / Fairly Efficient / Inefficient / Counterproductive

Q11.

> You are on your daily patrol, when a woman approaches you and your partner. The woman is very distressed.
>
> **Woman:** *'Please, officers, help me. My house has been broken into and they've taken loads of my possessions. They even stole my wedding ring. I'll bet it was those foreigners.'*

1. 'Okay, please calm down Madam. Unfortunately, there's not really much we can do.'

Efficient / Fairly Efficient / Inefficient / Counterproductive

2. 'Please try to calm down, Madam. We will conduct a thorough investigation of this incident. However, I will ask you to please retract your discriminatory comments.'

Efficient / Fairly Efficient / Inefficient / Counterproductive

3. 'Thank you for bringing this to our attention, Madam. We'll conduct a full investigation.'

Efficient / Fairly Efficient / Inefficient / Counterproductive

4. 'Your comments are discriminatory, and therefore we can't help you. Goodbye.'

Efficient / Fairly Efficient / Inefficient / Counterproductive

Q12.

> You have just finished your shift for the day, and you are walking back to your police car. Ahead of you, a young woman blows her nose, and then tosses the tissue on the floor, without turning around to pick it up.

1. Ignore it. You're off duty now.

Efficient / Fairly Efficient / Inefficient / Counterproductive

2. Call after the woman and reproach her for her behaviour. Warn her that behaviour such as this can lead to a penalty fine.

Efficient / Fairly Efficient / Inefficient / Counterproductive

3. Pick the tissue up and throw it in the bin.

Efficient / Fairly Efficient / Inefficient / Counterproductive

4. Inform the woman that you have no choice but to arrest her.

Efficient / Fairly Efficient / Inefficient / Counterproductive

Q13.

> You arrive at your desk to find that all of your paperwork for a certain case is missing. You have no idea where it's gone, but you know that a colleague has held a grudge against you ever since you started. What do you do?

1. Confront the colleague and demand that they tell you where they've hidden your paperwork.

Efficient / Fairly Efficient / Inefficient / Counterproductive

2. Remain calm and keep searching for your paperwork around your desk.

Efficient / Fairly Efficient / Inefficient / Counterproductive

3. Speak to your superior and accuse this colleague of hiding your work.

Efficient / Fairly Efficient / Inefficient / Counterproductive

4. Politely ask colleagues, including the one holding a grudge, if they've seen the paperwork that you've misplaced. If this doesn't work, speak to your superior.

Efficient / Fairly Efficient / Inefficient / Counterproductive

Q14.

You are on duty with a fellow officer and you come across a group of young people. They don't seem to be doing anything wrong, and aren't causing a nuisance to others in the area. They're all wearing hooded jumpers, but don't necessarily come across as threatening and aren't causing any trouble. Your fellow officer makes a judgement about them, telling them to move on. As they hesitate to move, the officer calls them 'thugs' and threatens to arrest them.

1. Proceed to arrest the young people.

Efficient / Fairly Efficient / Inefficient / Counterproductive

2. Pull your fellow officer to one side, telling her that she is behaving inappropriately.

Efficient / Fairly Efficient / Inefficient / Counterproductive

3. Say nothing, and turn a blind eye to your fellow officer.

Efficient / Fairly Efficient / Inefficient / Counterproductive

4. Tell the fellow officer that there's no reason to arrest the young people, and that she is unfairly discriminating against them because of the clothes that they're wearing and their age.

Efficient / Fairly Efficient / Inefficient / Counterproductive

Q15.

> **You are the desk sergeant at a local station. Your job is to deal with people who come in through the door/make enquiries at the desk. It is mid-morning, when a man approaches:**
>
> **Man:** *'My name is Jeff. I just discovered a dead body in my flat, but I have no idea how it got there. I don't know the victim and I didn't do it, I swear.'*

1. 'Please take a seat over there, I'll alert the chief investigator, who will be with you immediately.'

Efficient / Fairly Efficient / Inefficient / Counterproductive

2. 'Thank you for bringing this to our attention, sir. Do you know the name of the victim?'

Efficient / Fairly Efficient / Inefficient / Counterproductive

3. 'That's awful. How did they die?'

Efficient / Fairly Efficient / Inefficient / Counterproductive

4. 'Okay, thank you sir. We are going to need to ask you some important questions, and you may be detained. Do you understand this?'

Efficient / Fairly Efficient / Inefficient / Counterproductive

Q16.

> Your shift is about to end and you and your partner are heading back to the station in a police car. On the way, you get caught up in traffic. Your partner says, "Let's just turn on the sirens to get through this traffic quickly. We can even pass through the red light too, and get signed out and home as soon as possible." What do you do?

1. Proceed to activate the police sirens so that you can pass through the traffic.

Efficient / Fairly Efficient / Inefficient / Counterproductive

2. Remind your partner that this is an inappropriate use of the police sirens, and that they are reserved for real emergencies.

Efficient / Fairly Efficient / Inefficient / Counterproductive

3. Refuse to turn on the sirens yourself, but allow your partner to do it.

Efficient / Fairly Efficient / Inefficient / Counterproductive

4. Firmly say no, and then report his behaviour to your superior.

Efficient / Fairly Efficient / Inefficient / Counterproductive

Q17.

> You are set to go out on patrol with your partner for the day. However, when he turns up to the station, he is heavily intoxicated. You are the first person to see him. He is badly slurring his words, and unsteady on his feet.
>
> **Your partner:** *'C'mon mate...let's go start our shift. I've only had a couple...'*

1. Inform your partner that he needs to go home and sober up.

Efficient / Fairly Efficient / Inefficient / Counterproductive

2. Take your partner straight to the head of station. Behaviour like this is not acceptable.

Efficient / Fairly Efficient / Inefficient / Counterproductive

3. Take your partner out on shift with you, but keep a close eye on him.

Efficient / Fairly Efficient / Inefficient / Counterproductive

4. Drive your partner home, and then continue the shift by yourself.

Efficient / Fairly Efficient / Inefficient / Counterproductive

Q18.

> **You are out on patrol in the local neighbourhood, when a woman approaches you and your colleague. She is extremely angry, and using vulgar language.**
>
> **Woman:** *'Police scum. You can't trust Old Bill, all they do is cover up. When my house was burgled, the police did nothing! You two are good for nothing, waste of space.'*

1. 'Madam, your comments are totally unacceptable. Unless you have a real complaint, go away'

Efficient / Fairly Efficient / Inefficient / Counterproductive

2. Ignore her. She'll go away eventually.

Efficient / Fairly Efficient / Inefficient / Counterproductive

3. 'Excuse me, Madam, I will ask you to retract your comments. Language like that is not acceptable, and if you continue, we will have to detain you.'

Efficient / Fairly Efficient / Inefficient / Counterproductive

4. 'I'm sorry for the trouble that we have caused you. We'll do better next time to deal with your problems.'

Efficient / Fairly Efficient / Inefficient / Counterproductive

Q19.

> You are sitting in the canteen, discussing the morning's events with your colleague. You've had a difficult morning, after giving chase to a mugger on the high street. Unfortunately, the man got away.
>
> **You:** *'I was so close to catching him as well, I feel like I've let myself down. If that boy hadn't got in the way, I definitely could have got him.'*
>
> **In response, your colleague makes a homophobic remark.**

1. Laugh along with your colleague, it was just a joke.

Efficient / Fairly Efficient / Inefficient / Counterproductive

2. Inform your colleague that his comment is unacceptable, and that you will be taking this matter to the head of station.

Efficient / Fairly Efficient / Inefficient / Counterproductive

3. Reproach your colleague for his comment, and remind him that officers should be more respectful.

Efficient / Fairly Efficient / Inefficient / Counterproductive

4. Ask your colleague to think carefully about what he just said, and then change the topic of conversation.

Efficient / Fairly Efficient / Inefficient / Counterproductive

Q20.

It is the start of a new week, and you have been tasked with training a new staff member. Matthew is training to become a police officer. By the end of your first day, you are very pleased with Matthew's progress, and believe that he will make a great officer. Then, your senior officer approaches you:

Senior officer: *'So tomorrow, I'm going to put Matthew with someone else. From what I've seen, he's holding you back and getting in your way. Truth be told, it doesn't seem to me like he's got what it takes.'*

1. Inform your senior officer that you believe Matthew has great potential, but agree to his working with someone else.

Efficient / Fairly Efficient / Inefficient / Counterproductive

2. Agree with your senior officer. It's her decision, after all.

Efficient / Fairly Efficient / Inefficient / Counterproductive

3. Inform your senior officer that you would like to continue working with Matthew, and that you feel he has strong potential.

Efficient / Fairly Efficient / Inefficient / Counterproductive

4. Ask your senior officer to retract her comments. Inform her that you think she is being unfair and unprofessional.

Efficient / Fairly Efficient / Inefficient / Counterproductive

Q21.

You are on patrol with an officer in training, when you notice three youths sitting on a wall outside a house. All three youths are wearing school uniform. It's the middle of the day, and they are drinking from cans of alcohol. The area in question is an alcohol controlled area.

Officer in training: *'What should we do? Should we ignore them?'*

1. Approach the youths and ask them why they aren't in school.

Efficient / Fairly Efficient / Inefficient / Counterproductive

2. Ignore the youths. It's none of your business.

Efficient / Fairly Efficient / Inefficient / Counterproductive

3. Issue the youths with a penalty fine for drinking in an alcohol controlled area. Then start to investigate why they aren't in school.

Efficient / Fairly Efficient / Inefficient / Counterproductive

4. Ascertain the age of the youths, then issue them with a penalty fine for drinking, before asking them why they aren't in school.

Efficient / Fairly Efficient / Inefficient / Counterproductive

Q22.

> You are eating lunch in the canteen, when two of your religious colleagues make their way over to the corner of the room, and start praying. Another colleague loudly raises his voice, and says:
>
> **Colleague:** *'Can you stop that please? Do it somewhere else, this is a canteen!'*

1. Confront your colleague and ask him to leave the canteen. There is no place for discrimination in the police service.

Efficient / Fairly Efficient / Inefficient / Counterproductive

2. Concur with your colleague. The canteen is a place for eating, not for praying.

Efficient / Fairly Efficient / Inefficient / Counterproductive

3. Approach the religious individuals and inform them that they are more than welcome to pray in the canteen. Reproach your colleague for his comments.

Efficient / Fairly Efficient / Inefficient / Counterproductive

4. Approach your colleague and ask him to talk in private. Tell him that you believe his comments to the religious individuals are unfair.

Efficient / Fairly Efficient / Inefficient / Counterproductive

Q23.

You are due to begin your shift with a training candidate, at 9am. Unfortunately, by 5 minutes past 9, he still doesn't seem to have arrived at the station. When you go outside, you find him sleeping in his car.

1. Bang on the window and wake him up. 'You need to start your shift!'

Efficient / Fairly Efficient / Inefficient / Counterproductive

2. Go straight to your senior officer, and report the candidate. Behaviour like this is not acceptable.

Efficient / Fairly Efficient / Inefficient / Counterproductive

3. Wake the candidate up and then have a serious chat with him. Tell him that unfortunately you will need to report this to your senior officer.

Efficient / Fairly Efficient / Inefficient / Counterproductive

4. Leave him sleeping. You can handle the shift on your own.

Efficient / Fairly Efficient / Inefficient / Counterproductive

Q24.

> You are working on the desk at police HQ, when a woman comes in through the door. She appears to be fairly distressed:
>
> **Woman:** *'No…speak bad English. I don't understand. Please, help.'*

1. Tell the woman that you cannot help her if she is unable to explain herself properly.

Efficient / Fairly Efficient / Inefficient / Counterproductive

2. Ask the woman to take a seat and you will contact someone who can assist her.

Efficient / Fairly Efficient / Inefficient / Counterproductive

3. Ask the woman if she could talk a little louder.

Efficient / Fairly Efficient / Inefficient / Counterproductive

4. Try to calm the woman down, before speaking to her slowly and clearly, and trying to establish clues from her language.

Efficient / Fairly Efficient / Inefficient / Counterproductive

Q25.

> You are policing a local festival, when you notice a young man slumped against the wall. The man appears to be intoxicated, and is drooling from the mouth.

1. Approach the man and attempt to find out his name. Ask around to see if he has any friends in the vicinity.

Efficient / Fairly Efficient / Inefficient / Counterproductive

2. Immediately radio for the nearest ambulance, and stay with the man until it arrives.

Efficient / Fairly Efficient / Inefficient / Counterproductive

3. Try and pick the man up, and escort him to the nearest ambulance.

Efficient / Fairly Efficient / Inefficient / Counterproductive

4. Ask the man if he can stand up. If he can't, place him under arrest for being drunk and disorderly.

Efficient / Fairly Efficient / Inefficient / Counterproductive

Q26.

It's the end of your shift, and you are in a rush because you have a birthday party to attend during the evening. As you pack your things away for the day, one of the trainee officers approaches you:

Trainee Officer: *'Hi, I know you are nearly finished for the day, but I just wondered if you could take a quick look at this case report for me? I filled it in but I didn't want to submit it without getting it checked first, just in case I missed anything.'*

1. Ask the officer to find someone else to help him, as you are finished work for the day.

Efficient / Fairly Efficient / Inefficient / Counterproductive

2. Sit down with the trainee and go through the case report, making sure he's included all of the essential details.

Efficient / Fairly Efficient / Inefficient / Counterproductive

3. Tell the trainee that you are confident in his ability to file a good case report, and that he should just submit it.

Efficient / Fairly Efficient / Inefficient / Counterproductive

4. Take a quick look over the case report, and give the trainee some tips, before heading off for the evening.

Efficient / Fairly Efficient / Inefficient / Counterproductive

Q27.

> You are patrolling with two new trainees, when the two get into a disagreement. Things start to escalate, and before you know it, the two are squaring up to each other.
>
> **Trainee one:** *'Get out of my face, mate.'*
>
> **Trainee two:** *'Fam, I'll put you to sleep.'*

1. Immediately step between the two individuals and try to calm the situation.

Efficient / Fairly Efficient / Inefficient / Counterproductive

2. Inform the two individuals that they are acting extremely unprofessionally, and that you will need to report this incident to the head of station.

Efficient / Fairly Efficient / Inefficient / Counterproductive

3. Let the two individuals fight it out. It's character building.

Efficient / Fairly Efficient / Inefficient / Counterproductive

4. Confront trainee two for his aggression. Threats are totally unacceptable.

Efficient / Fairly Efficient / Inefficient / Counterproductive

Q28.

> You are working at the local football stadium. You and your colleague have been tasked with checking bags on individuals entering the stadium, on a random basis. Halfway through your shift, your colleague starts to argue with an entrant.
>
> **Man:** *'Oh, so you think I look like a criminal, do you? Didn't check the guy in front of me, maybe it's just because of the colour of my skin. Is that it? You're a racist!'*

1. 'Please, calm down sir. We are requested to check individuals based on whether we think they look suspicious. In this case, my partner has every right to examine your bag.'

Efficient / Fairly Efficient / Inefficient / Counterproductive

2. 'You are being extremely aggressive sir. If you don't calm down, we will have to detain you.'

Efficient / Fairly Efficient / Inefficient / Counterproductive

3. 'This is a standard security check, sir. Please calm down so that we can check your bag.'

Efficient / Fairly Efficient / Inefficient / Counterproductive

4. 'Our security checks are conducted at random, sir. It has nothing to do with the colour of your skin.'

Efficient / Fairly Efficient / Inefficient / Counterproductive

Q29.

You are policing a local shopping centre, when a disgruntled woman approaches you:

Woman: *'There's a man with a dog walking around on the top floor. I thought animals weren't allowed in this centre? The man is blind, but I'm scared of dogs. You need to ask him to remove the dog from the premises.'*

The centre's policy clearly states that dogs are allowed, if they are assisting disabled persons.

1. 'I'm very sorry about that, Madam. I'll contact the security service and get them on the case.'

Efficient / Fairly Efficient / Inefficient / Counterproductive

2. 'While it's true that this centre does not allow animals on the premises, we do make an exception for disabled individuals, who would otherwise not be able to attend without these animals. For this reason, I cannot help you with this matter.'

Efficient / Fairly Efficient / Inefficient / Counterproductive

3. 'Guide dogs are permitted. I believe that you are being quite ignorant in this regard, Madam.'

Efficient / Fairly Efficient / Inefficient / Counterproductive

4. 'Madam, I'm sure you can understand that guide dogs are essential in some circumstances. For this reason, I cannot help you.'

Efficient / Fairly Efficient / Inefficient / Counterproductive

Q30.

You are policing the local neighbourhood. As you walk past the park, you notice a group of school boys playing a football match. Someone flies in with a late tackle, and suddenly a scuffle breaks out. Two of the boys are on the floor, punching each other.

1. Separate the two boys, and then ask them to leave the premises.

Efficient / Fairly Efficient / Inefficient / Counterproductive

2. Wait until the fight is finished, and then warn both boys about their bad behaviour.

Efficient / Fairly Efficient / Inefficient / Counterproductive

3. Separate the two boys, and warn them that violence is not a way to solve disputes.

Efficient / Fairly Efficient / Inefficient / Counterproductive

4. Arrest both of the boys. Fighting in public is not acceptable.

Efficient / Fairly Efficient / Inefficient / Counterproductive

Q31.

You are just finishing your shift for the day. As you drive through the local neighbourhood, you notice a car parked by the side of the road. The car is in an unusual position, in what would normally be considered a no-parking zone. You approach the car. There is a man slumped back against the driver's side seat. You do not know whether he is sleeping, or seriously injured.

1. Knock on the window. If you get no response, call the emergency services.

Efficient / Fairly Efficient / Inefficient / Counterproductive

2. Leave the man to it. He's probably sleeping.

Efficient / Fairly Efficient / Inefficient / Counterproductive

3. Smash the car window. The man could be in serious trouble.

Efficient / Fairly Efficient / Inefficient / Counterproductive

4. Knock several times on the window. If you get no response, call police HQ and ask them to check who the car's license plate belongs to.

Efficient / Fairly Efficient / Inefficient / Counterproductive

Q32.

You are policing a local football match. Just before the match is about to start, a fight breaks out between two rival fans at the gate. A man wearing a red shirt jumps on a man wearing a blue shirt, catching him unawares, and starts hitting him. He then pokes him in the eye. The man in the blue shirt is not acting aggressively, and just trying to get away. After the fight is broken up, it's left to you to decide what to do.

1. Ask both men to go with your fellow officer to the station, to give a statement.

Efficient / Fairly Efficient / Inefficient / Counterproductive

2. Place the man in the red shirt under arrest. Check whether the man in the blue shirt requires medical assistance, before granting him access to the stadium.

Efficient / Fairly Efficient / Inefficient / Counterproductive

3. Arrest both men. Violent behaviour is unacceptable.

Efficient / Fairly Efficient / Inefficient / Counterproductive

4. Give both men a caution, and then allow them into the stadium, separately.

Efficient / Fairly Efficient / Inefficient / Counterproductive

Q33.

> You are on the way to your shift at the local station, but get stuck in traffic. A sign above the motorway indicates that you are going to be delayed well beyond your starting time.

1. Call the station and let them know about the situation. Promise to be in as soon as possible.

Efficient / Fairly Efficient / Inefficient / Counterproductive

2. Call your colleague and ask him to cover the start of your shift.

Efficient / Fairly Efficient / Inefficient / Counterproductive

3. Just get into work when you can. It's not your fault if there's traffic.

Efficient / Fairly Efficient / Inefficient / Counterproductive

4. Call the head of station on his mobile. It's best to let him know as soon as possible.

Efficient / Fairly Efficient / Inefficient / Counterproductive

Q34.

> You are policing a local shopping centre. As you walk past a shop, a young man standing outside confronts you. He seems extremely disgruntled. After a short verbal exchange, he spits in your face.

1. Punch the man and pin him to the floor. You have a right to defend yourself.

Efficient / Fairly Efficient / Inefficient / Counterproductive

2. Grab the man and place him under arrest. This is totally unacceptable behaviour.

Efficient / Fairly Efficient / Inefficient / Counterproductive

3. Walk away from the situation. You don't need to deal with people like this.

Efficient / Fairly Efficient / Inefficient / Counterproductive

4. Radio for backup, and warn the man that his actions will have serious consequences.

Efficient / Fairly Efficient / Inefficient / Counterproductive

Q35.

> You are working a shift with your partner, when you suddenly start to feel extremely ill. You feel dizzy and lethargic, and it becomes harder and harder to concentrate.
>
> **Colleague:** *'Are you okay? Don't worry, we've only got an hour left.'*

1. Ask your colleague if she would feel comfortable finishing the shift on her own.

Efficient / Fairly Efficient / Inefficient / Counterproductive

2. Tell your colleague that it's okay, you'll finish the shift.

Efficient / Fairly Efficient / Inefficient / Counterproductive

3. Ask your colleague if it's possible to take a break and sit down for a bit.

Efficient / Fairly Efficient / Inefficient / Counterproductive

4. Call police HQ and ask them if they are okay for you to finish early.

Efficient / Fairly Efficient / Inefficient / Counterproductive

Q36.

You are working with a trainee officer. At the end of the day, as you sort through paperwork, you notice that the trainee has made a big mistake. Unfortunately, he has already gone home.

1. Correct his mistake and pretend it never happened. You haven't got time for him to amend it himself.

Efficient / Fairly Efficient / Inefficient / Counterproductive

2. Highlight the error, in pencil, and then leave the paperwork on his desk, for the next morning. He needs to learn from his mistakes.

Efficient / Fairly Efficient / Inefficient / Counterproductive

3. Correct his mistake but sit down with him in the next morning to talk about the error.

Efficient / Fairly Efficient / Inefficient / Counterproductive

4. Call him on his mobile to let him know about his error. Inform him that you are extremely disappointed.

Efficient / Fairly Efficient / Inefficient / Counterproductive

Q37.

> **You are working on patrol with two trainee officers. As you walk down the street, you notice an extremely expensive car parked by the side of the road. The trainee officers get very excited, and run over to take pictures with the car.**
>
> **Trainee 1:** *'Wow, what a nice car. Let me take a selfie!'*
>
> **Trainee 2:** *'Don't worry, I'll take it for you. Say cheese!'*

1. Admonish the trainee officers for their unprofessional behaviour. Tell them that this is not acceptable for police officers.

Efficient / Fairly Efficient / Inefficient / Counterproductive

2. Laugh along with the trainees, but ask them to come away from the car, and stop them from taking pictures of it.

Efficient / Fairly Efficient / Inefficient / Counterproductive

3. Call Police HQ, reporting the trainees immediately. Demand that they are removed from the force.

Efficient / Fairly Efficient / Inefficient / Counterproductive

4. Tell the trainees that they need to delete any images they take of the car.

Efficient / Fairly Efficient / Inefficient / Counterproductive

Q38.

You are responding to a callout, as backup for an officer who is in serious trouble. Whilst travelling to the location, your partner demands that you pull over and stop outside a restaurant, so he can run in and grab something to eat.

1. Refuse to pull over. Tell your partner that this could be a life and death situation, and that he can eat afterwards.

Efficient / Fairly Efficient / Inefficient / Counterproductive

2. Explain to your partner why this isn't the right course of action. If he persists, pull over and let him out. Then drive to the callout by yourself.

Efficient / Fairly Efficient / Inefficient / Counterproductive

3. Ask your partner whether he can grab you some chips.

Efficient / Fairly Efficient / Inefficient / Counterproductive

4. Radio ahead to ask whether you are urgently needed at the scene, and if it's okay for you to stop for food.

Efficient / Fairly Efficient / Inefficient / Counterproductive

Q39.

> **You arrive into work at 5 to 9. Your shift will start at 9am. When you arrive in, the desk sergeant approaches you:**
>
> **Desk sergeant:** *'Hey, can you pop down to the shops and pick up some milk, please? We've run out and nobody can have tea.'*

1. 'Sorry, my shift begins in 5 minutes, and I need to prepare for it. You'll have to find someone else.'

Efficient / Fairly Efficient / Inefficient / Counterproductive

2. 'I don't drink tea, so you'll have to find someone else to do it.'

Efficient / Fairly Efficient / Inefficient / Counterproductive

3. 'That's fine, but I'll be late for my shift. Hopefully that's okay.'

Efficient / Fairly Efficient / Inefficient / Counterproductive

4. 'Let me ask the head of station if it's okay for me to go. If so, sure, I'd be happy to.'

Efficient / Fairly Efficient / Inefficient / Counterproductive

Q40.

> **You are sitting in the canteen, when your colleague approaches you. He sits down at your table and says the following:**
>
> **Colleague**: *'Lately I've been feeling very down. Although I'm on medication, I've been having thoughts about taking my own life. I feel very alone. You are the first person I've told about this, so please keep it a secret.'*

1. Inform your colleague that he can always talk to you in confidence, but that you will need to report what he has said, out of concern for his safety.

Efficient / Fairly Efficient / Inefficient / Counterproductive

2. Tell your colleague that you'll keep his secret, and that he can always talk to you when he's feeling down.

Efficient / Fairly Efficient / Inefficient / Counterproductive

3. Ask your colleague whether there is any way that he can obtain therapy, as suicide is not the answer.

Efficient / Fairly Efficient / Inefficient / Counterproductive

4. Ask your colleague not to disclose personal information to you. It's none of your business.

Efficient / Fairly Efficient / Inefficient / Counterproductive

Q41.

> You have been working with your partner for a number of weeks now. Over the weeks, you have observed that your partner is in a fairly poor physical condition. He appears out of breath when required to exert himself, and frequently needs to take rest breaks. He also seems to have put on weight.

1. Sit down with your partner and tell him that you are concerned about his health. Demand that he cuts back on the fast food.

Efficient / Fairly Efficient / Inefficient / Counterproductive

2. Set up a meeting with your partner and the head of station, to discuss your concerns.

Efficient / Fairly Efficient / Inefficient / Counterproductive

3. Go straight to the head of station. Your partner has violated the expectations of the police, and needs to be removed at once.

Efficient / Fairly Efficient / Inefficient / Counterproductive

4. Sit down with your partner and elaborate on your concerns. Ask him whether there is anything you can do to help him.

Efficient / Fairly Efficient / Inefficient / Counterproductive

Q42.

You are policing a local station, when a dispute breaks out between two women.

Woman 1: *'She stole my bag!'*

Woman 2: *'She's lying, it's my bag! I bought it last week!'*

Woman 1: *'You lying little trollop!'*

1. Arrest woman 2 on charges of theft. Take her back to the station for questioning.

Efficient / Fairly Efficient / Inefficient / Counterproductive

2. Confiscate the bag, and tell both women that they will need to come back with you, where you'll analyse the CCTV footage.

Efficient / Fairly Efficient / Inefficient / Counterproductive

3. Tell the two women to take their dispute elsewhere. You don't have time to deal with petty squabbles.

Efficient / Fairly Efficient / Inefficient / Counterproductive

4. Confiscate the bag, and take the details of the two women. Tell them that the police will be in touch.

Efficient / Fairly Efficient / Inefficient / Counterproductive

Q43.

> You are just finishing up for the day, when one of your colleagues approaches you. She has something confidential that she wants to share:
>
> **Colleague:** *'Hi mate. Just to let you know, I think I saw Perkins going through your drawer while you were out for lunch earlier. Did you give him permission for that?'*

1. Inform your colleague that no, you did not give Perkins permission. Take this matter straight to the head of station.

Efficient / Fairly Efficient / Inefficient / Counterproductive

2. Ask your colleague whether she is completely sure of what she saw. Then, ask to speak to Perkins alone.

Efficient / Fairly Efficient / Inefficient / Counterproductive

3. Accuse your colleague of making up stories. Perkins would never do that.

Efficient / Fairly Efficient / Inefficient / Counterproductive

4. Ask your colleague to clarify the exact time at which this incident occurred. Then, check your desk to see if anything is missing.

Efficient / Fairly Efficient / Inefficient / Counterproductive

Q44.

You are going back to your desk at the station, when you overhear a conversation from around the corner. The conversation is between two of your colleagues:

Colleague 1: *'That's right, and if you tell anyone, I'll knock you out. You understand that? Snitches get stitches.'*

Colleague 2: *'Please, get off me. I won't say anything.'*

Both colleagues swiftly exit the scene.

1. Find colleague 2 and tell him that you overheard the conversation. Demand to know what is going on.

Efficient / Fairly Efficient / Inefficient / Counterproductive

2. Ignore it. It's none of your business.

Efficient / Fairly Efficient / Inefficient / Counterproductive

3. Tell your senior manager what you have heard. He is best placed to deal with this.

Efficient / Fairly Efficient / Inefficient / Counterproductive

4. Locate colleague 2 and tell him that colleague 1's behaviour is unacceptable. Ask him to come with you to the head of station.

Efficient / Fairly Efficient / Inefficient / Counterproductive

Q45.

You are patrolling a local neighbourhood, when you receive a call from police HQ, with regards to gunshots heard from a local house. You and your partner find the door of the property open, and a man (who works for the police) dead inside. The killer is hiding in the kitchen. You catch, neutralise and handcuff him. Then your partner says:

Partner: *'This scumbag is a police killer. Before we take him back to the station, let's teach him a lesson!'*

1. Tell your partner that as much as the man disgusts you, you cannot break the law yourselves. Call the station and let them know about the situation.

Efficient / Fairly Efficient / Inefficient / Counterproductive

2. Tell your partner that you'll be waiting outside in the car. Leave him to it.

Efficient / Fairly Efficient / Inefficient / Counterproductive

3. Advise your partner that such behaviour would be breaking the law, but that you won't stand in his way.

Efficient / Fairly Efficient / Inefficient / Counterproductive

4. Tell your partner that such behaviour would only lower him to the criminal's level. Urge him to think sensibly.

Efficient / Fairly Efficient / Inefficient / Counterproductive

Q46.

> You are on evening patrol in a local neighbourhood. As you walk past a house, you notice that music is blaring extremely loudly from an open window. The music is so loud that it can be heard from the other end of the street.

1. Knock on the door and politely ask the homeowner to turn the music down. You don't want to be dealing with a noise complaint.

Efficient / Fairly Efficient / Inefficient / Counterproductive

2. Ignore it. When someone makes a noise complaint, you'll deal with the situation.

Efficient / Fairly Efficient / Inefficient / Counterproductive

3. Bang on the door, and demand that the homeowner lowers the volume of the music.

Efficient / Fairly Efficient / Inefficient / Counterproductive

4. Knock on the doors of the houses next to the property. Ask the residents if the noise is bothering them.

Efficient / Fairly Efficient / Inefficient / Counterproductive

Q47.

> Your head of station has asked to speak to you at the end of the day. You can't recall if you've done anything wrong, but you are extremely nervous. What do you do?

1. Ask someone more senior than yourself whether they have any idea what he wants to talk to you about.

Efficient / Fairly Efficient / Inefficient / Counterproductive

2. Go and knock on his office door earlier, just to make sure you haven't done anything wrong.

Efficient / Fairly Efficient / Inefficient / Counterproductive

3. Leave early, so that you don't have to deal with him until tomorrow.

Efficient / Fairly Efficient / Inefficient / Counterproductive

4. Look through your recent case report history, just in case he wants to discuss any of this with you. It's best to be prepared.

Efficient / Fairly Efficient / Inefficient / Counterproductive

Q48.

> You are just finishing up for the day, when the head of station approaches you. He claims that earlier on, you left the station evidence locker open and unsecured. You quickly realise that you've made a big mistake.

1. Feign ignorance. There's no need for you to risk your job over something so trivial.

Efficient / Fairly Efficient / Inefficient / Counterproductive

2. Own up to the mistake, but tell the head of station that somebody else should have made sure the locker was secured.

Efficient / Fairly Efficient / Inefficient / Counterproductive

3. Apologise for the error and assure the head of station that it won't happen again.

Efficient / Fairly Efficient / Inefficient / Counterproductive

4. Apologise for the error, and ask the head of station for tips on how you can make sure this doesn't happen again.

Efficient / Fairly Efficient / Inefficient / Counterproductive

Q49.

You have been tasked with ensuring that no members of the public cross the perimeter of an established crime scene. Likewise, the head of station has asked officers to refrain from talking to the local media regarding the crime. As you stand watch, you notice that one of your colleagues is in conversation with a journalist.

Colleague: *'Yeah, so the body was found over there…*points*…and the victim was aged 42, male.'*

1. Take your colleague to one side and remind him of what the head of station said.

Efficient / Fairly Efficient / Inefficient / Counterproductive

2. Step in and immediately put a halt to the interview. Inform your colleague that he needs to ring police HQ immediately, to inform them of what he's just done.

Efficient / Fairly Efficient / Inefficient / Counterproductive

3. Step in and put a stop to the interview. Send the journalist away, before calling police HQ to inform them of the situation.

Efficient / Fairly Efficient / Inefficient / Counterproductive

4. Ask the journalist to leave immediately. Tell your colleague that he must not share information with anyone else.

Efficient / Fairly Efficient / Inefficient / Counterproductive

Q50.

> **You are working with a close colleague, whom you have known for a number of years. As you patrol the local neighbourhood, you notice a woman with a very visible tattoo on her arm, displaying her allegiance to a prominent nationalist party.**
>
> **Colleague:** *'That's despicable. Let's arrest her.'*

1. Inform your colleague that although he might not agree with the woman's views, there are no grounds to arrest her.

Efficient / Fairly Efficient / Inefficient / Counterproductive

2. Inform your colleague that it's important to be respectful of everybody's views, regardless of whether he agrees with them. Place the woman under arrest.

Efficient / Fairly Efficient / Inefficient / Counterproductive

3. Tell your colleague that he needs to be more accepting of alternative viewpoints. Encourage him to go and speak to the woman about her tattoo.

Efficient / Fairly Efficient / Inefficient / Counterproductive

4. Ignore your colleague. He's entitled to his own views, but you won't be placing anyone under arrest.

Efficient / Fairly Efficient / Inefficient / Counterproductive

Non-Specific Police Situational Judgement: Practice Test 2

Test 2 contains 30 practice questions. Answers on page 156.

Q1.

> You are working in an office when a member of staff, who is in a wheelchair, approaches you. She asks you if you would be willing to swap desks, as your desk is closer to the exit route, and it will make it easier for her to go to the toilet when required. How do you react?

1. Say no. You are already settled in at your desk and to move would cause unnecessary upheaval.

Efficient / Fairly Efficient / Inefficient / Counterproductive

2. Say yes. This is not a problem for you and you can see why moving desks would help her out and improve her working day.

Efficient / Fairly Efficient / Inefficient / Counterproductive

3. Tell her to speak to your boss first, to see if he is in agreement with her request. If he doesn't have a problem with it, neither do you.

Efficient / Fairly Efficient / Inefficient / Counterproductive

4. Tell her you would be willing to swap desks providing she is prepared to move all of your belongings to the new desk.

Efficient / Fairly Efficient / Inefficient / Counterproductive

Q2.

You are a train conductor working on your local line. At 10 past 10 in the morning, you are performing your hourly ticket inspection. You come across a man on the train who has not purchased a ticket. He claims that the reason for this is because he had to board the train quickly. It's an emergency as his mother has taken a fall and is in hospital. He has the money to pay the fare there and then. His station is two stops away. What do you do?

1. Consult with the other people in the carriage as to what to do.

Efficient / Fairly Efficient / Inefficient / Counterproductive

2. Allow him to pay the full ticket fare to his intended stop.

Efficient / Fairly Efficient / Inefficient / Counterproductive

3. Perform a citizen's arrest. This man is a criminal.

Efficient / Fairly Efficient / Inefficient / Counterproductive

4. Issue the man with a standard penalty fare.

Efficient / Fairly Efficient / Inefficient / Counterproductive

Q3.

> Your company has recently hired a new staff member. He has only been working for you for 2 days, but you have noticed him making inappropriate remarks towards female staff members. Your manager does not seem to have noticed. One of your female colleagues has confessed that his behaviour makes her feel uncomfortable, but she does not want to risk jeopardising the employee's future, especially since he has only just joined the company. Another female staff member claims that the next time he does it, she will 'give him a smack'. What do you do?

1. Take the new employee to one side and tell him that his behaviour needs to change.

Efficient / Fairly Efficient / Inefficient / Counterproductive

2. Go to your manager and explain the situation.

Efficient / Fairly Efficient / Inefficient / Counterproductive

3. Encourage your female colleagues to speak to your manager.

Efficient / Fairly Efficient / Inefficient / Counterproductive

4. Ignore the behaviour. He's only joking.

Efficient / Fairly Efficient / Inefficient / Counterproductive

Q4.

> You have been working in a hugely successful company for the past 10 years. Recently, however, your company's fortunes seem to have taken a turn for the worse. Profits are at an all-time low, employees seem to be drastically underperforming and your sales manager refuses to accept any of the blame. He claims that the bad results are out of his control, and that the products being produced are simply of poor quality. Privately, he has also informed you that he believes customers are being scared off by current employee sales techniques, and as a result won't purchase from the organisation. During a recent team meeting, one of your colleagues tried to raise her concerns. Your sales manager lambasted her, branding her weak and naïve. Your colleague was extremely upset by this behaviour, and is considering making a complaint of sexism to the chairman of the company. Although in your opinion there is no evidence to suggest this, she has asked you to act as a witness to her statement. What do you do?

1. Agree to act as a witness, but tell the chairman that there is no evidence to suggest sexism.

Efficient / Fairly Efficient / Inefficient / Counterproductive

2. Tell the chairman that you believe your sales manager was acting in a sexist manner.

Efficient / Fairly Efficient / Inefficient / Counterproductive

3. Agree to act a witness. Suggest to the chairman that the department needs some extra help.

Efficient / Fairly Efficient / Inefficient / Counterproductive

4. Encourage your colleague to sue the company. Sexism is unacceptable.

Efficient / Fairly Efficient / Inefficient / Counterproductive

Q5.

You are working for a train company as a platform assistant. Part of your job is to assist disabled passengers on and off the train. It is the middle of a weekday, and therefore there are very few customers to deal with. On the other side of the platform, you notice a well-known celebrity. One of your colleagues has noticed this too, and suggests that you both go over to the other side to get her autograph. What do you do?

1. Agree to cross over and get an autograph. This could be your only chance to meet such a prestigious person.

Efficient / Fairly Efficient / Inefficient / Counterproductive

2. Tell your colleague that you won't be going anywhere. What they do is up to them.

Efficient / Fairly Efficient / Inefficient / Counterproductive

3. Refuse to go, and encourage your colleague to do the same. This would be unprofessional.

Efficient / Fairly Efficient / Inefficient / Counterproductive

4. Take mobile pictures of the celebrity from afar, but don't approach them.

Efficient / Fairly Efficient / Inefficient / Counterproductive

Q6.

You are the customer service assistant in a shopping centre. Two men approach you, arguing furiously. One of the men approaches you, claiming that the other man took his bag. The other man says that the bag was his all along, and that the first man is lying. He states 'finder's keepers'. You ask the man to hand over the bag to you, so that the CCTV footage of the centre can be reviewed. This leaves the first man irate. As you turn around to deal with him, the second man runs off with the bag, jumps into a taxi, and is gone. What do you do?

1. Offer to take the man's contact details, so that he can be reimbursed for the price of some of his shopping.

Efficient / Fairly Efficient / Inefficient / Counterproductive

2. Tell the man there is nothing that can be done. You snooze, you lose.

Efficient / Fairly Efficient / Inefficient / Counterproductive

3. Report the incident to senior management. Tell the man that your company will be in touch.

Efficient / Fairly Efficient / Inefficient / Counterproductive

4. Take the man into a private room where you can write up a report of the incident, which will then be passed on to the police.

Efficient / Fairly Efficient / Inefficient / Counterproductive

Q7.

You are working as a barista in a coffee shop. Every Tuesday, a man comes in your shop at 10am. You have noticed that he wears a wedding ring. He sits at the same table, in the same seat, every time. The man often brings female companions with him, and appears very affectionate to all of them. In the past 2 months, you have seen the man kiss at least 5 different women. You suspect him of cheating. What do you do?

1. Ignore the situation. It's none of your business.

Efficient / Fairly Efficient / Inefficient / Counterproductive

2. Confront the man on the spot. Cheating is immoral.

Efficient / Fairly Efficient / Inefficient / Counterproductive

3. Take the man to one side and quietly ask him to explain his behaviour.

Efficient / Fairly Efficient / Inefficient / Counterproductive

4. Talk to your colleague about your concern, this is a good outlet.

Efficient / Fairly Efficient / Inefficient / Counterproductive

Q8.

You are the centre manager for a well-known writing retreat in the English countryside. Part of your role is ensuring that the centre is well staffed, food goes out on time and that the centre is kept clean and tidy. You have recently taken on a new staff member, who is struggling with his position. Today you have discovered that the new staff member has forgotten to pre-order food supplies, meaning that there is no way to cook dinner for the course attendees that evening. The staff member is fairly upset at his mistake. What do you say to him?

1. 'Pack your bags. You're sacked.'

Efficient / Fairly Efficient / Inefficient / Counterproductive

2. 'Mistakes happen. Let's pull the team together and brainstorm some ideas as to how we can fix this.'

Efficient / Fairly Efficient / Inefficient / Counterproductive

3. 'Maybe you should consider whether this is the right position for you.'

Efficient / Fairly Efficient / Inefficient / Counterproductive

4. 'Okay, obviously this isn't ideal, but let's think of some solutions. We'll have a serious chat about this at the end of the day though.'

Efficient / Fairly Efficient / Inefficient / Counterproductive

Q9.

You are the manager of a major sporting retail store. The previous day, one of your staff members was using a ladder to retrieve an item for a customer. Due to incorrect safety precautions, the ladder fell, injuring the staff member. She has broken her ankle, and therefore won't be in work for a significant period of time. It is your job to call her the next day. What do you say to her?

1. 'Hi. I'm really sorry about the incident that occurred yesterday. We hope to see you back at work soon.'

Efficient / Fairly Efficient / Inefficient / Counterproductive

2. 'Hi. Unfortunately, since you are part time, and can no longer work, we are going to have to terminate your contract.'

Efficient / Fairly Efficient / Inefficient / Counterproductive

3. 'Hi. Do you think you could come in and work on crutches?'

Efficient / Fairly Efficient / Inefficient / Counterproductive

4. 'Hi. I'm really sorry about the incident that took place at work yesterday. I'd like to assure you that we will conduct a full investigation of the incident, to ensure it doesn't happen again.'

Efficient / Fairly Efficient / Inefficient / Counterproductive

Q10.

You are a staff member at a care home. You recently took a week off for a relative's funeral. Upon your return to the care home, you hear that your manager has been gossiping about you behind your back, with the other staff at the care home. According to your source, your manager questioned the necessity of taking 5 days off for a funeral, and called you lazy. You are upset by these claims. What do you do?

1. Spread bad rumours about your manager. Two can play that game.

Efficient / Fairly Efficient / Inefficient / Counterproductive

2. Take your manager to one side and question her on whether the claims are true. Explain why you needed the time off.

Efficient / Fairly Efficient / Inefficient / Counterproductive

3. Arrange a team meeting to try and get to the bottom of this.

Efficient / Fairly Efficient / Inefficient / Counterproductive

4. Ring your manager in your own time to try and discuss the situation further.

Efficient / Fairly Efficient / Inefficient / Counterproductive

Q11.

> You are working as a shop assistant in a toy shop. A woman approaches you and asks for help locating a particular brand of toy. She informs you that the toy is showing 'IN STOCK' on the company website and that she has travelled 10 miles to buy it. After searching for 10 minutes you establish that the toy is out of stock and the information on the website is incorrect. What would you do?

1. Apologise to the customer and say you are sorry but there is nothing more you can do.

Efficient / Fairly Efficient / Inefficient / Counterproductive

2. Apologise to the customer and inform her that there is another toy shop 15 miles away in the next town. If she travels there, they might have the toy she wants in stock.

Efficient / Fairly Efficient / Inefficient / Counterproductive

3. Apologise unreservedly for the toy not being in stock. Tell her that you will order the toy immediately from your supplier and then deliver it to her home as soon as it arrives. She will not be charged for either the toy or the delivery due to the inconvenience and stress caused.

Efficient / Fairly Efficient / Inefficient / Counterproductive

4. Apologise unreservedly for the toy not being in stock. Tell her that you will order the toy immediately from your supplier and then deliver it to her home as soon as it arrives. She will be charged for the toy, but not for the delivery, due to the inconvenience and stress caused.

Efficient / Fairly Efficient / Inefficient / Counterproductive

Q12.

You are working as a delivery driver for a well-known supermarket delivering food to customers' homes. Whilst attending someone's home to deliver their food order, they offer you £10 as a thank you for being prompt and for giving an excellent service. The company has a strict policy which states that you must not take any form of tip or financial reward from customers whilst at work. What would you do?

1. Thank them for the money, put it in your pocket, and leave a happy person. Nobody will ever know that you took the money, so there's no harm.

Efficient / Fairly Efficient / Inefficient / Counterproductive

2. Thank them for the money, but explain that you are unable to accept tips or financial rewards of this nature. Tell them that if they would like to give a reward, the supermarket supports local charities and they will be able to donate via their website.

Efficient / Fairly Efficient / Inefficient / Counterproductive

3. Thank them for their kind offer, but explain that you are unable to accept tips or financial rewards of this nature.

Efficient / Fairly Efficient / Inefficient / Counterproductive

4. Walk away and ignore them.

Efficient / Fairly Efficient / Inefficient / Counterproductive

Q13.

> You are working as a Health and Safety assessor and are visiting a local warehouse to talk to the staff about risk assessments. Whilst walking around the warehouse you notice that a number of the fire doors are wedged open illegally. What do you do?

1. Ignore it. You are at the premise to talk to the staff about a specific subject and it would be inappropriate to say anything there and then.

Efficient / Fairly Efficient / Inefficient / Counterproductive

2. Remove the wedges yourself and then report the situation to the local Fire Safety Officer when you return to your office later that day. He/she can then carry out a formal inspection.

Efficient / Fairly Efficient / Inefficient / Counterproductive

3. Inform the responsible person at the warehouse that the wedges need to be moved immediately. Then, once you return to the office you will report the matter to your local Fire Safety Officer so that he/she can carry out a thorough inspection of the premise.

Efficient / Fairly Efficient / Inefficient / Counterproductive

4. Remove the wedges holding the doors open yourself and say nothing more about it.

Efficient / Fairly Efficient / Inefficient / Counterproductive

Q14.

> During an office meeting your line manager is explaining a number of changes that are being introduced to the working day. These changes will mean that you and your work colleagues will have more tasks to complete during the working day. The majority of other members of the team start to make their objections to the changes heard. What would you do?

1. Join in with the objections. Why change things when everything is going OK as it is?

Efficient / Fairly Efficient / Inefficient / Counterproductive

2. Keep your head down. Whilst you don't agree with the changes you don't want to get into trouble for raising your concerns.

Efficient / Fairly Efficient / Inefficient / Counterproductive

3. Accept the changes yourself. It doesn't matter what the others think. After all, they are entitled to their own opinion.

Efficient / Fairly Efficient / Inefficient / Counterproductive

4. Accept the changes. Change is part of working life. You would also try and explain the benefit of the changes to those who are skeptical.

Efficient / Fairly Efficient / Inefficient / Counterproductive

Q15.

You are working as a bus driver and it is coming to the end of your shift. In 5 minutes' time, you are due to sign off and head home. Your line manager approaches you and asks you to mop the bus depot floor before you go off duty. You realise that this will take you 15 minutes to do the job professionally. What would you do?

1. Carry out the task as requested, professionally, even though it will mean that you have to stay behind at work for an additional 10 minutes.

Efficient / Fairly Efficient / Inefficient / Counterproductive

2. Inform your manager that you are happy to complete the task, but ask if you can finish slightly earlier tomorrow to compensate.

Efficient / Fairly Efficient / Inefficient / Counterproductive

3. Carry out the task to a slightly lesser standard, therefore finishing your shift on time.

Efficient / Fairly Efficient / Inefficient / Counterproductive

4. Politely refuse to carry out the task.

Efficient / Fairly Efficient / Inefficient / Counterproductive

Q16.

> You are managing a team of six people at a distribution centre.
> It is approaching the annual peak time for business where your
> staff will need to be at their best in order to cope with demand.
> You are concerned as all of your staff have been making careless
> mistakes whilst dispatching goods, due to increased workload.
> What would you do?

1. Get the team together and tell them that, if matters do not improve, you will speak to the main boss about getting them replaced.

Efficient / Fairly Efficient / Inefficient / Counterproductive

2. Hold a team meeting as soon as possible to establish the reasons why so many mistakes are being made. Then, formulate and agree a plan with all of the team in order to improve performance.

Efficient / Fairly Efficient / Inefficient / Counterproductive

3. Get stuck in yourself more to help the team out. Clearly they are very busy and they could do with an extra pair of hands.

Efficient / Fairly Efficient / Inefficient / Counterproductive

4. Speak to your boss and explain to her that you need to take on another member of staff to ease the pressure on the team.

Efficient / Fairly Efficient / Inefficient / Counterproductive

Q17.

You are working as a retail assistant in a high street store. It is a very busy day in the shop and everyone is working flat out serving and helping customers. You are walking towards the back of the shop through the storage area to take your 10 minute tea break, when you notice that the contents of a large shelf have all fallen on the floor. You estimate it would take you at least 10 minutes to put all of the contents back on the shelf. What would you do?

1. Walk around the contents and go for your tea break. You are legally entitled to a break and someone else will be able to clear up the mess.

Efficient / Fairly Efficient / Inefficient / Counterproductive

2. Inform your manager that you are going to put the contents back on the shelf and request that you take your 10 minute tea break after the job is complete.

Efficient / Fairly Efficient / Inefficient / Counterproductive

3. Inform your manager that the contents have fallen on the floor, and ask him if he can find someone else to put the contents back on the shelf, as you are about to go on your tea break.

Efficient / Fairly Efficient / Inefficient / Counterproductive

4. Forget about your tea break and put the contents back on the shelf yourself.

Efficient / Fairly Efficient / Inefficient / Counterproductive

Q18.

You are working alone as a barista at a local coffee shop. It is a Saturday morning and there is a large queue of people waiting to be served. All of a sudden the coffee machine breaks down and you will be unable to serve coffee for the rest of the day. You will still be able to serve soft drinks and tea. What would you do?

1. Apologise to the people in the queue and inform them you will not be able to serve them due to the breakdown of the coffee machine, which is beyond your control. Then, close the shop and make your way home.

Efficient / Fairly Efficient / Inefficient / Counterproductive

2. Apologise to the people in the queue and inform them that you will only be able to serve soft drinks and tea due to the breakdown of the coffee machine. Then, create a sign that says 'COFFEE MACHINE BROKEN – WE ARE ONLY ABLE TO SERVE SOFT DRINKS AND TEA – APOLOGIES FOR ANY INCONVENIENCE CAUSED' and place it on the shop door so that people can make a decision whether or not they want to come in.

Efficient / Fairly Efficient / Inefficient / Counterproductive

3. Apologise to each person as they reach the front of the queue and explain to them that you are unable to serve coffee but that you can serve them soft drinks or tea.

Efficient / Fairly Efficient / Inefficient / Counterproductive

4. Call your boss and ask her what she wants you to do.

Efficient / Fairly Efficient / Inefficient / Counterproductive

Q19.

> You are a supervisor for a small business and you have been carrying out interviews for a new role within the company. You interviewed 4 people for the new role and one of them has been successful. After you write rejection letters to the 3 candidates who were unsuccessful, one of them arrives at your office to complain. He says he is bitterly disappointed in the fact he was not successful and wants an explanation from you. What would you do?

1. Tell him you are not obliged to go into reasons why he was not successful, and ask him to leave.

Efficient / Fairly Efficient / Inefficient / Counterproductive

2. Provide him with a short list of reasons for why he was unsuccessful, and encourage him to apply for future positions.

Efficient / Fairly Efficient / Inefficient / Counterproductive

3. Listen to his concerns and allow him to vent his frustrations. Once he has finished, explain to him that there is a robust and thorough selection process in place and that unfortunately, on this occasion, he was unsuccessful and that someone else was found more suitable for the role. Then, offer him constructive feedback on his performance during the interview.

Efficient / Fairly Efficient / Inefficient / Counterproductive

4. Invite him to sit down and make him a cup of tea. Whilst you are out of the office, call your boss and ask for advice on how to deal with the situation.

Efficient / Fairly Efficient / Inefficient / Counterproductive

Q20.

> You are working as a retail shop assistant and it is your turn to work on the customer services desk. A man, who appears to be angry, approaches you with an electric shaver in his hand. He tells you that he only bought the shaver from your shop three weeks ago but that it has now stopped working completely. He wants a replacement to be provided. The shop has a 28-day refund/exchange policy providing a receipt can be supplied. He does not have a receipt. What would you do?

1. Apologise for the inconvenience that has been caused through the defective shaver. Explain to the customer the company's refund policy and that a receipt is required for a refund or exchange. However, explain to him that, if he can provide proof of purchase, by way of a card statement, that you will ask your manager if you can exchange the shaver for him.

Efficient / Fairly Efficient / Inefficient / Counterproductive

2. Explain to him that, because he does not have a receipt, you are not able to help him.

Efficient / Fairly Efficient / Inefficient / Counterproductive

3. Apologise for the inconvenience that has been caused through the defective shaver and then happily exchange the defective shaver for a new one.

Efficient / Fairly Efficient / Inefficient / Counterproductive

4. Ask your manager what he thinks you should do.

Efficient / Fairly Efficient / Inefficient / Counterproductive

Q21.

You are a supervisor working for a large corporate organisation. You are in a meeting with your manager along with ten other supervisors. Your manager has a very strong accent different to your own and tends to talk quickly, often making it difficult for people to understand her. So far, during the meeting, you have not been able to understand most of what she has been saying. What would you do?

1. As soon as there becomes a natural break in her talk, raise your hand and explain that you are finding it difficult to understand most of what she is saying. Respectfully ask if she would please slow down so that you can take in all of the important information she is relaying.

Efficient / Fairly Efficient / Inefficient / Counterproductive

2. Wait to the end of the meeting and then ask your work colleagues for clarification on what she was saying.

Efficient / Fairly Efficient / Inefficient / Counterproductive

3. Wait to the end of the meeting before speaking to her in private and explain to her that you didn't understand most of what she was saying.

Efficient / Fairly Efficient / Inefficient / Counterproductive

4. Do nothing

Efficient / Fairly Efficient / Inefficient / Counterproductive

Q22.

> You have just started a new job as a manager with a large corporate company. On your first day at work another manager approaches you and starts telling you negative things about your boss. She tells you that he is very poor at doing his job and that you shouldn't trust him as he tends to speak about his staff behind their backs. What would you do?

1. Challenge her in a respectable manner and say that you think she is wrong for saying these things about a senior member of the team.

Efficient / Fairly Efficient / Inefficient / Counterproductive

2. Thank her for the information and be on your guard from now on when dealing with your manager.

Efficient / Fairly Efficient / Inefficient / Counterproductive

3. Thank her for the information but explain that you do not want to pre-judge people and you want to have an entirely open mind. You will take him as you find him.

Efficient / Fairly Efficient / Inefficient / Counterproductive

4. Thank her for the information and then ask other people within the organisation if they have had the same experience whilst working with your manager.

Efficient / Fairly Efficient / Inefficient / Counterproductive

Q23.

You are a manager of a hotel chain and you receive a call from your managing director at head office. She has requested that you spend the day managing at another hotel twenty-five miles away as the current manager there has gone off sick. You have a large amount of paperwork to catch up on and you intended on doing it today whilst working at your own hotel. What would you do?

1. Explain that you cannot meet their request as you have lots of paperwork work to catch up on.

Efficient / Fairly Efficient / Inefficient / Counterproductive

2. Explain to head office that you have lots of paperwork to catch up on and ask them how they want you to prioritise your work.

Efficient / Fairly Efficient / Inefficient / Counterproductive

3. Tell head office that you have lots of paperwork to catch up on but that you are prepared to ring around the other hotels in the region to see if there is another manager available to go to the hotel. If not, then you would be prepared to go and you would have to catch up with your paperwork another time.

Efficient / Fairly Efficient / Inefficient / Counterproductive

4. Agree to go to the hotel for the rest of the day and take your paperwork with you to do, whilst you are there.

Efficient / Fairly Efficient / Inefficient / Counterproductive

Q24.

> You are working as an admin assistant in a typical office environment when you can't help overhearing your manager reprimanding one of your work colleagues for poor performance. Your manager is clearly not happy with your colleague and he is making it perfectly clear that he expects to see rapid improvement. You are concerned for your work colleague as he hasn't been himself lately, and you can see that something has been troubling him. What would you do?

1. Speak to your colleague in private and ask him whether anything is wrong. You would also offer your support to see if you can help him through this difficult period he is going through.

Efficient / Fairly Efficient / Inefficient / Counterproductive

2. Approach your manager in confidence and tell him that you think there might be something wrong with your work colleague, which is ultimately having an impact on his work performance.

Efficient / Fairly Efficient / Inefficient / Counterproductive

3. Do nothing. You do not want to interfere as it is not your problem.

Efficient / Fairly Efficient / Inefficient / Counterproductive

4. Speak to your work colleague and offer to do some of his work for him in order to ease the pressure he is under from his manager.

Efficient / Fairly Efficient / Inefficient / Counterproductive

Q25.

> You are a supervisor working in a warehouse and it is 30 minutes until your shift ends. The oncoming shift supervisor calls you and tells you he is going to be 30 minutes late as he is stuck in traffic. You have a dinner date booked with your girlfriend that evening and you need to get away. What would you do?

1. Tell the oncoming shift workers that they will have to work on their own, unsupervised, for 30 minutes until their supervisor arrives.

Efficient / Fairly Efficient / Inefficient / Counterproductive

2. Call your girlfriend and tell her you will be late coming home. Then, supervise the oncoming shift workers until their supervisor arrives.

Efficient / Fairly Efficient / Inefficient / Counterproductive

3. Call your boss and ask her what she thinks you should do.

Efficient / Fairly Efficient / Inefficient / Counterproductive

4. Just leave at the end of your shift. The fact that he is going to be late is not your problem.

Efficient / Fairly Efficient / Inefficient / Counterproductive

Q26.

You have been working in a new team for 3 months now. When you started, your line manager put you on a 6-month development programme where you would be closely supervised for that period of time. You now feel very much ready to work alone and the close supervision is starting to frustrate you and hinder your development. What would you do?

1. Complete the 6-month supervision period as planned and don't say anything about how you feel.

Efficient / Fairly Efficient / Inefficient / Counterproductive

2. Tell your work colleagues how you feel and get their advice on what they think you should do.

Efficient / Fairly Efficient / Inefficient / Counterproductive

3. Start working more on your own without telling anyone.

Efficient / Fairly Efficient / Inefficient / Counterproductive

4. Arrange a meeting with your line manager to explain how you now feel ready to work more on your own, unsupervised. Ask for his permission for the supervision period to come to an end.

Efficient / Fairly Efficient / Inefficient / Counterproductive

Q27.

You are the supervisor of a small team working for an online mail order company. It is December and it's the busiest time of the year. Your team is snowed under with work and some of the team members are clearly feeling the strain. You have a team development meeting booked for the forthcoming Tuesday morning. However, one of the team members approaches you and tells you that she won't be at the meeting as she is too busy to attend. What would you do?

1. Spend time with the team member to identify ways in which she can manage her time more efficiently so that she can attend the team development meeting.

Efficient / Fairly Efficient / Inefficient / Counterproductive

2. Tell the team member that the team development meeting is mandatory. She must attend.

Efficient / Fairly Efficient / Inefficient / Counterproductive

3. Tell the team member that you understand how she is feeling and that she does not need to attend the team development meeting.

Efficient / Fairly Efficient / Inefficient / Counterproductive

4. Get a member of staff from another team to cover the team member's workload during the day of the meeting so that she can attend.

Efficient / Fairly Efficient / Inefficient / Counterproductive

Q28.

> You have noticed one of your colleagues continuously turning up to work with a hangover. You haven't said anything before, but you've realised that the situation is becoming more frequent. Today at work, the same colleague has turned up to work, and you can smell alcohol on their breath. The colleague is disruptive, loud, and is clearly still intoxicated. What would you do?

1. You tell your colleague that he is being extremely unprofessional and tell him to arrange a lift home and sober up.

Efficient / Fairly Efficient / Inefficient / Counterproductive

2. You inform your colleague that you are aware of the said issue, and encourage him to seek help.

Efficient / Fairly Efficient / Inefficient / Counterproductive

3. You get another one of your colleagues to drive him home, so you can continue working in peace.

Efficient / Fairly Efficient / Inefficient / Counterproductive

4. You tell him to make a cup of coffee and sober up, and get on with his work quietly.

Efficient / Fairly Efficient / Inefficient / Counterproductive

Q29.

> You are the project manager of a team of 5. Your group has been tasked with analysing and correlating key intelligence information which has been passed on to you by another sector, before sending it off to management. Halfway through the project, one of your team members approaches you, claiming that she no longer wants to work with another member of the team. The reason for this is that she believes the person in question has been undermining her and making sarcastic comments directed at her. You have not heard anything of this sort. The individual threatening to leave the team is highly experienced and her absence would severely damage the group's chances of success. What would you do?

1. Explain to your team member that the group needs her, and that she should rise above it and continue with the project.

Efficient / Fairly Efficient / Inefficient / Counterproductive

2. Wait to see if you hear anything as mentioned by the individual, and then take action.

Efficient / Fairly Efficient / Inefficient / Counterproductive

3. Sit the individual in question down, and ask their side of the story.

Efficient / Fairly Efficient / Inefficient / Counterproductive

4. Sit them both down to try and resolve the issue, before continuing on with the project.

Efficient / Fairly Efficient / Inefficient / Counterproductive

Q30.

You have just finished creating an important presentation that is being presented this afternoon. You show it to your boss and ask for their feedback. Whilst he says he is impressed with the overall layout and design of the presentation, he has a few concerns. He feels as though the presentation is lacking in statistics and financial data, which is crucial to this presentation's success. You know that adding this information is going to take time, and you are not sure if you have enough research to go on to add this information in such short notice. What would you do?

1. Explain to your boss that the presentation is being presented that afternoon, and ask him for ideas on how to implement this information in time.

Efficient / Fairly Efficient / Inefficient / Counterproductive

2. Inform your boss that whilst you cannot add in this information due to time constraints, you will be happy to answer any questions they have.

Efficient / Fairly Efficient / Inefficient / Counterproductive

3. Ignore your boss's concerns and present the presentation the way it is.

Efficient / Fairly Efficient / Inefficient / Counterproductive

4. Ask your colleagues to help you with the additional information, so that you can ensure the work gets added.

Efficient / Fairly Efficient / Inefficient / Counterproductive

Suggested Answers:
Test 1

Q1.

1. Help the man to his feet, apologise for knocking him over, put the t-shirt back in his bag for him and wish him a good day.

Answer: Inefficient

Explanation: The reason that this answer is inefficient, is that you are not resolving the issue. Instead, you are simply ignoring it and letting the man leave.

2. Help the man to his feet and examine the t-shirt. Place him under arrest, then conduct a stop and search for a receipt for the t-shirt and question the man on where he got it from.

Answer: Fairly Efficient

Explanation: The reason that is answer is fairly efficient, is that you are taking steps to deal with the problem. However, this approach is overreacting and you don't yet have cause to place the man under arrest..

3. Ask the man to come with you to the security office, so that you can investigate further. Explain to him that this is a precautionary step.

Answer: Efficient

Explanation: The reason that this answer is efficient, is that you are taking all of the necessary steps to resolve the issue, including explaining to the man why you have taken this course of action.

4. Pin the man to the floor and proceed to arrest him.

Answer: Counterproductive

Explanation: The reason that this is counterproductive is because you are immediately jumping to (aggressive) conclusions about the man's behaviour. It could well be a mistake. Pinning him to the floor should be a last resort, when all other potential avenues have been exhausted.

Q2.

1. Inform your colleague that you have the utmost respect for him, regardless of his sexual preferences, and that his secret is safe with you.

Answer: Efficient

Explanation: The reason that this answer is efficient is because you are showing your colleague respect/demonstrating a good level of tolerance, and helping him to gain trust in you by assuring him that the information will remain confidential.

2. Inform your colleague that there is no reason to be ashamed of this, and encourage him to tell other people at the station

Answer: Inefficient.

Explanation: The reason that this answer is inefficient, is that you are encouraging the individual to go around telling other people at the station, when this is not a matter that needs to be discussed. Whatever the man's sexual preferences, this is not an appropriate topic of conversation in the workplace, and is only acceptable in this circumstance because he has confided in you. Casually discussing the issue with everyone else at the station is unnecessary.

3. Inform your colleague that there is no place for people like him in the police force, and that he should hand in his badge.

Answer: Counterproductive

Explanation: This is counterproductive, because you are showing extreme intolerance, and making the individual feel unwelcome. Also, the statement that you are making is completely untrue. The police service does not discriminate.

4. Inform your colleague that his secret is safe with you, before changing the topic of conversation.

Answer: Fairly Efficient

Explanation: The reason that this is fairly efficient is because you are assuring your colleague of your confidentiality, and then changing the conversation onto something more appropriate for the workplace environment.

Q3.

1. 'It's okay, we'll just have to proceed without those documents for now. Hopefully they won't be too important.'

Answer: Inefficient

Explanation: The reason that this answer is inefficient is because the documents are important, and that it's likely you will need them later down the line. In this answer, you are simply ignoring the problem.

2. 'This is a disaster. You've derailed the entire investigation. I'm afraid you're sacked.'

Answer: Counterproductive

Explanation: The reason that this is counterproductive is because in this answer, you are taking extremely rash and unnecessary action. Furthermore, based on the role that this question gives you (senior officer) there is no indication that you have the power to remove people from their job.

3. 'Okay, don't panic. I'll contact the senior administrator, who should have photocopies of the forms. Later this afternoon though we'll have a serious chat about this.'

Answer: Efficient

Explanation: The reason that this response is efficient, is because you are offering a solution to the problem, calming the individual down, and informing them that there could be repercussions for their mistake.

4. 'Can you explain to me how this happened? This is a very serious incident.'

Answer: Fairly Efficient

Explanation: The reason that this response is fairly efficient, is because you are taking a serious approach to this problem, and identifying to the individual that it needs to be dealt with.

Q4.

1. Inform your fellow officer that they are acting very unprofessionally, and tell them to get back to work.

Answer: Efficient

Explanation: This is the most efficient response. You are clearly indicating to your partner that they are not acting in an acceptable manner, and are encouraging them to focus on the job at hand – policing.

2. Leave your fellow officer to it. It's not your problem if they want to mess around.

Answer: Inefficient

Explanation: This is inefficient, as you are simply ignoring the issue.

3. Inform your fellow officer that you'll be reporting them to your head of station for this.

Answer: Fairly Efficient

Explanation: This is fairly efficient, albeit perhaps a little unnecessary. In this instance, your colleague's unprofessional behaviour could be dealt with by giving them a stern warning, rather than immediately escalating the matter to the head of station.

4. Laugh. They are only having a bit of fun.

Answer: Counterproductive.

Explanation: This is counterproductive. By laughing, you are encouraging their behaviour.

Q5.

1. Ignore it. He's probably just forgotten his keys.

Answer: Inefficient

Explanation: The reason that this is inefficient, is because you aren't doing anything to act upon a potentially serious situation. At the very least, you need to question the man.

2. Immediately call the station to ask for backup. You may need help to apprehend the criminal.

Answer: Fairly Efficient

Explanation: This is a fairly efficient response, as you are taking steps to secure your own safety, and to deal with the problem. That being said, it's entirely possible that this is just a misunderstanding, and in any case your new partner is due to arrive shortly.

3. Wait for the man to exit the property, and then confront him.

Answer: Efficient

Explanation: This is an efficient response. Instead of going charging in, assuming the worst, wait for the man to exit the property. This means that you can deal with him in a calm and professional manner.

4. Immediately attempt to enter the property yourself. You need to stop the man before he gets away.

Answer: Counterproductive

Explanation: This is a rash and potentially damaging decision, especially if the person turns out to be the homeowner/has just forgotten their keys. Furthermore, in attempting to enter the property yourself (by force) you will probably end up damaging the house.

Q6.

1. 'I'll have to ask my senior officer about that, give me a moment.'

Answer: Inefficient

Explanation: This is inefficient, as you already know that members of the public are not allowed inside the perimeter. Therefore, you would be wasting the time of both yourself and your senior officer by asking him.

2. 'Sure, go right ahead, just tell them that I let you in.'

Answer: Counterproductive

Explanation: This is counterproductive, as you are completely breaking the rules. It's a crime scene, meaning the public cannot enter.

3. 'I'm sorry sir but this is a crime scene, we can't allow anyone to enter.'

Answer: Efficient

Explanation: This is a crime scene, meaning that members of the public are absolutely not allowed in. The most efficient response is to politely but firmly deny the man entrance.

4. 'Since your bag has been left at the scene, it could be used as evidence. For this reason, I'm afraid I can't retrieve it for you.'

Answer: Fairly Efficient

Explanation: This is a fairly efficient response, as it tells the person why they cannot have their bag back. However, it does not explain that members of the public are not allowed on the crime scene.

Q7.

1. 'If you say please.'

Answer: Counterproductive

Explanation: This is rude/disrespectful to your superior.

2. 'I'll do my best, although I've got a lot of paperwork to complete. Would you prefer me to prioritise this form?'

Answer: Efficient

Explanation: This is efficient, as you are assuring the officer that you will do your best to complete the task, whilst also giving them an explanation for why it might be difficult.

3. 'No chance, you'll have to wait until tomorrow.'

Answer: Inefficient

Explanation: Not only is this quite rude, but you are giving no attempt or effort to try and get the work completed, nor are you even providing an explanation.

4. 'Sure, I'll give it immediate priority.'

Answer: Fairly Efficient

Explanation: This is a fairly efficient response, although it does not take into account the other work that you need to do.

Q8.

1. Inform your fellow officer that it's your duty to protect the public, and immediately intervene.

Answer: Efficient

Explanation: As a police officer, you have a duty of care for the public. You need to step in and stop this fight from escalating even further.

2. Allow your fellow officer to call for backup, while trying to intervene yourself.

Answer: Fairly Efficient

Explanation: This is fairly efficient, as at least you are intervening in the fight. However, something of this nature should really not require more than two of you (unless things seriously escalate) and therefore it's better if your partner assists you in intervening.

3. Agree with your fellow officer. There's no point putting yourself in danger.

Answer: Counterproductive

Explanation: As a police officer, you have a duty of care to the public. By refusing to intervene, you are neglecting this duty.

4. Encourage your fellow officer to intervene, while you call for backup.

Answer: Inefficient

Explanation: Although this is technically the same as option 2, encouraging your partner to intervene whilst you make the call to the station is not particularly bold on your part; particularly as your partner believes that you should ignore the fight altogether.

Q9.

1. 'Alright, bye.'

Answer: Inefficient.

Explanation: This is inefficient, as you are simply allowing your partner to leave, without resolving the issue.

2. 'You've finished early a few times recently. Your shift isn't meant to end till 5pm.'

Answer: Efficient

Explanation: This is an efficient response, as you are calling your partner out on his questionable behaviour.

3. 'I'm going to tell police HQ about this.'

Answer: Fairly Efficient

Explanation: This is fairly efficient, as you are making an effort to resolve the situation. However, it's entirely possible that your partner hasn't realised they've been finishing early, so it's worth discussing with them first, before going to police HQ about the issue.'

4. 'Our shift doesn't finish for another half an hour. Get back here, or else…'

Answer: Counterproductive

Explanation: This is counterproductive. The use of the phrase 'or else' implies a threat, making this unacceptable behaviour.

Q10.

1. Approach the shopkeeper and inform him that you believe someone has just stolen from his store.

Answer: Efficient

Explanation: This is an efficient response. The shopkeeper can confirm whether or not the individual has paid. If he hasn't, you should then have time to apprehend him.

2. Ignore the situation. The man has probably paid.

Answer: Counterproductive

Explanation: This is counterproductive, as you are simply ignoring the issue.

3. Follow the man out of the shop and question him.

Answer: Fairly Efficient

Explanation: This is a fairly efficient response. You are taking direct action to deal with the problem. However, it's better to approach the shopkeeper first, before assuming the worst about the individual.

4. Ask the shopkeeper if you can take a look at the shop's CCTV footage.

Answer: Inefficient

Explanation: This is an inefficient response. There are no grounds for you to look at the CCTV footage, especially not before ascertaining whether the man has stolen.

Q11.

1. 'Okay, please calm down Madam. Unfortunately there's not really much we can do.'

Answer: Inefficient

Explanation: This is an inefficient response. You are failing to reassure the woman that the police will deal with the issue, and therefore damaging the reputation of the service.

2. 'Please try to calm down, Madam. We will conduct a thorough investigation of this incident. However, I will ask you to please retract your discriminatory comments.'

Answer: Efficient

Explanation: This is an efficient response, as it reassures the woman that the police will deal with the issue, but also rebukes her for her discriminatory remarks.

3. 'Thank you for bringing this to our attention, Madam. We'll conduct a full investigation.'

Answer: Fairly Efficient

Explanation: This is a fairly efficient response. Although you are reassuring the woman that action will be taken, you are failing to address her discrimination.

4. 'Your comments are discriminatory, and therefore we can't help you. Goodbye.'

Answer: Counterproductive

Explanation: This is counterproductive. Although you are addressing the woman's discrimination, this type of response will only serve to make her angrier, and make the situation worse. Although her discrimination should not be accepted, this does not mean that the police can't help her.

Q12.

1. Ignore it. You're off duty now.

Answer: Inefficient

Explanation: This is inefficient, as you are not taking action over a blatant infringement of the law. Regardless of whether you are on duty, as a policeman it is your responsibility to deal with issues such as this.

2. Call after the woman and reproach her for her behaviour. Warn her that behaviour such as this can lead to a penalty fare.

Answer: Efficient

Explanation: This is an efficient response to this situation. You are informing the woman in no uncertain terms that her behaviour is unacceptable, and about the potential repercussions of this.

3. Pick the tissue up and throw it in the bin.

Answer: Fairly Efficient

Explanation: This is a fairly efficient response. You are removing the litter, but failing to reproach the woman for her behaviour.

4. Inform the woman that you have no choice but to arrest her.

Answer: Counterproductive

Explanation: This is an extreme overreaction and you have no grounds to arrest the woman for this.

Q13.

1. Confront the colleague and demand that they tell you where they've hidden your paperwork.

Answer: Counterproductive

Explanation: This is an overreaction, and you have no evidence to support your theory that this colleague has stolen your work. You'd also likely be causing a disturbance in the office.

2. Remain calm and keep searching for your paperwork around your desk.

Answer: Fairly Efficient

Explanation: This is fairly efficient because you may have just misplaced your work. However, you might also be wasting precious time.

3. Speak to your superior and accuse this colleague of hiding your work.

Answer: Inefficient

Explanation: This is better than publicly confronting your colleague and disrupting others, but is still inefficient because you have no evidence other than a hunch to prove that they've stolen from you.

4. Politely ask colleagues, including the one holding a grudge, if they've seen the paperwork that you've misplaced. If this doesn't work, speak to your superior.

Answer: Efficient

Explanation: This is the best solution as it's possible that someone had to move your paperwork throughout the day. Also, one of your colleagues might have seen the grudge-holding colleague steal your paperwork.

Q14.

1. Proceed to arrest the young people.

Answer: Counterproductive

Explanation: These young people aren't breaking the law and arresting them is just acting on your fellow officer's prejudice towards them.

2. Pull your fellow officer to one side, telling her that she is behaving inappropriately.

Answer: Fairly Efficient

Explanation: This is fairly efficient because you are stopping your fellow officer from treating these civilians in an inappropriate manner.

3. Say nothing, and turn a blind eye to your fellow officer.

Answer: Inefficient

Explanation: By allowing your fellow officer to continue wrongfully accosting the young people, you are implicitly saying that her behaviour is acceptable.

4. Tell the fellow officer that there's no reason to arrest the young people, and that she is unfairly discriminating against them because of the clothes that they're wearing and their age.

Answer: Efficient

Explanation: This is the best solution because, not only are you stopping your fellow officer from continuing, but you're also letting them know *why* their behaviour is unacceptable.

Q15.

1. 'Please take a seat over there. I'll alert the chief investigator, who will be with you immediately.'

Answer: Efficient

Explanation: This is an efficient response, as you are giving the matter serious concern, and treating it with priority. You are alerting the right person, who can deal with it as soon as possible.

2. 'Thank you for bringing this to our attention, sir. Do you know the name of the victim?'

Answer: Inefficient

Explanation: The individual has already said that they don't know the victim.

3. 'That's awful. How did they die?'

Answer: Counterproductive.

Explanation: This is unprofessional and does not help the situation.

4. 'Okay, thank you sir. We are going to need to ask you some important questions, and you may be detained. Do you understand this?'

Answer: Efficient

Explanation: This is a fairly efficient response. You are clearly laying out the seriousness of the incident, and providing the individual with key facts on the protocol from this point onwards.

Q16.

1. Proceed to activate the police sirens so that you can pass through the traffic.

Answer: Counterproductive

Explanation: This is an inappropriate use of police equipment for one's personal gain. The sirens should only be used in emergencies.

2. Remind your partner that this is an inappropriate use of the police sirens, and that they are reserved for real emergencies.

Answer: Efficient

Explanation: This is the best response because you're not only telling your partner that this is unacceptable, but also *why* it's wrong to do so.

3. Refuse to turn on the sirens yourself, but allow your partner to do it.

Answer: Inefficient

Explanation: Even though you aren't turning on the sirens yourself, you're responsible for the behaviour of both yourself and your partner while on duty.

4. Firmly say no, and then report his behaviour to your superior.

Answer: Fairly Efficient

Explanation: This is a fairly efficient response because you're stopping your partner from behaving inappropriately and you're also letting your superiors know about the situation.

Q17.

1. Inform your partner that he needs to go home and sober up.

Answer: Fairly Efficient

Explanation: This is a fairly efficient response. You are not allowing your partner to work with you, as he is clearly not in a fit state.

2. Take your partner straight to the head of station. Behaviour like this is not acceptable.

Answer: Efficient

Explanation: This is the most efficient response. It is totally unacceptable for your partner to turn up to work in this state, and the matter needs to be dealt with by the head of station.

3. Take your partner out on shift with you, but keep a close eye on him.

Answer: Counterproductive

Explanation: This is a counterproductive response. Your partner is clearly unfit to perform police work, and taking him out with you would only cause further problems. You need to report this immediately.

4. Drive your partner home, and then continue the shift by yourself.

Answer: Inefficient

Explanation: This is inefficient. Not only do you need to report this to the head of station, but it is impractical and unsafe to perform a shift by yourself. At the very least, you will need to find a new partner for the day.

Q18.

1. 'Madam, your comments are totally unacceptable. Unless you have a real complaint, go away.'

Answer: Fairly Efficient

Explanation: This is a fairly efficient response. You are dismissing the woman's comments, and making it clear that they are unacceptable.

2. Ignore her. She'll go away eventually.

Answer: Inefficient

Explanation: This is an inefficient response. The woman is verbally abusing officers of the law, and making unfounded accusations. At the very least, she needs to be made clear that what she is saying is wrong.

3. 'Excuse me, Madam, I will ask you to retract your comments. Language like that is not acceptable, and if you continue, we will have to detain you.'

Answer: Efficient

Explanation: This is an efficient response, as you are clearly telling the woman that her behaviour is unacceptable, and providing her with a serious warning.

4. 'I'm sorry for the trouble that we have caused you. We'll do better next time to deal with your problems.'

Answer: Counterproductive.

Explanation: This is counterproductive, as you are simply accepting the unfounded accusations of the woman.

Q19.

1. Laugh along with your colleague, it was just a joke.

Answer: Counterproductive

Explanation: This is counterproductive, as by laughing along, you are sending the message that this type of behaviour is correct.

2. Inform your colleague that his comment is unacceptable, and that you will be taking this matter to the head of station.

Answer: Efficient

Explanation: This is efficient. There is no room for discrimination within the police service and any homophobic comments must be dealt with accordingly.

3. Reproach your colleague for his comment, and remind him that officers should be more respectful.

Answer: Fairly Efficient

Explanation: This response is fairly efficient, as you are personally addressing the issue and reinforcing that homophobic comments are unacceptable.

4. Ask your colleague to think carefully about what he just said, and then change the topic of conversation.

Answer: Inefficient

Explanation: This is a inefficient response, as although you have highlighted the comment and changed the topic of conversation, you have not challenged your colleague to change their behaviour.

Q20.

1. Inform your senior officer that you believe Matthew has great potential, but agree to his working with someone else.

Answer: Fairly Efficient

Explanation: This is a fairly efficient response. You are clearly correcting the officer on his judgement of Matthew, but at the same time are reaching a compromise/not going against his instructions.

2. Agree with your senior officer. It's her decision, after all.

Answer: Inefficient

Explanation: This is an inefficient response. You are ignoring your own judgement of the situation, and letting the senior officer maintain an opinion that is (in your view) incorrect.

3. Inform your senior officer that you would like to continue working with Matthew, and that you feel he has strong potential.

Answer: Efficient

Explanation: This is an efficient response. The question clearly indicates that you are pleased with Matthew's progress. Therefore, this is what you should tell your senior officer.

4. Ask your senior officer to retract her comments. Inform her that you think she is being unfair and unprofessional.

Answer: Counterproductive

Explanation: This is a big overreaction. It's entirely possible that your senior officer has simply made a mistake, which you can easily correct him on, without being insulting.

Q21.

1. Approach the youths and ask them why they aren't in school.

Answer: Inefficient

Explanation: This is inefficient. It's not enough to simply ask the youths why they aren't in school. Although this is a concern, the bigger concern should be over them drinking in a public area, and whether they are of legal age to be consuming alcohol in the first place.

2. Ignore the youths. It's none of your business.

Answer: Counterproductive

Explanation: This is a counterproductive response. This is not a situation that you can simply ignore.

3. Issue the youths with a penalty fine for drinking in an alcohol controlled area. Then start to investigate why they aren't in school.

Answer: Fairly Efficient

Explanation: This is a fairly efficient response, albeit not as strong as it could be. It's important to ascertain whether the youths are of legal age to be drinking in the first place, as well as the other considerations.

4. Ascertain the age of the youths, then issue them with a penalty fine for drinking, before asking them why they aren't in school.

Answer: Efficient

Explanation: This is an efficient response, as it takes into account all of the options available to you, and doesn't miss any lines of enquiry.

Q22.

1. Confront your colleague and ask him to leave the canteen. There is no place for discrimination in the police service.

Answer: Inefficient

Explanation: This is an inefficient response, as you aren't really dealing with the problem. You need to explain to your colleague why his comments are wrong, instead of simply kicking him out.

2. Concur with your colleague. The canteen is a place for eating, not for praying.

Answer: Counterproductive

Explanation: This is a counterproductive response, as you are demonstrating similar discrimination to your colleague. This is unacceptable.

3. Approach the religious individuals and inform them that they are more than welcome to pray in the canteen. Reproach your colleague for his comments.

Answer: Efficient

Explanation: This is the most efficient response to the situation. You are clearly showing that discriminatory behaviour will not be tolerated, and that the police force as a whole has an acceptance of religious requirements and individuals.

4. Approach your colleague and ask him to talk in private. Tell him that you believe his comments to the religious individuals are unfair.

Answer: Fairly Efficient

Explanation: This is a fairly efficient response, as it clearly shows your colleague that his behaviour was wrong. However, you also need to show your religious colleagues that his behaviour is not representative of the entire police force.

Q23.

1. Bang on the window and wake him up. "You need to start your shift!"

Answer: Inefficient

Explanation: It's not enough to just wake the officer up, you need to try and understand his behaviour, and then report it.

2. Go straight to your senior officer, and report the candidate. Behaviour like this is not acceptable.

Answer: Fairly Efficient

Explanation: This is a fairly efficient response to the scenario. However, the best response would be to talk with the officer beforehand, to try and understand his behaviour.

3. Wake the candidate up and then have a serious chat with him. Tell him that unfortunately you will need to report this to your senior officer.

Answer: Efficient

Explanation: This is the most efficient response to this scenario. Although you could go straight to your senior officer, it is best to wake the trainee officer first, to explain to him the seriousness of the situation.

4. Leave him sleeping. You can handle the shift on your own.

Answer: Counterproductive

Explanation: You should not be expected to deal with a shift on your own, simply because your partner has overslept/is late for work. This is counterproductive.

Q24.

1. Tell the woman that you cannot help her if she is unable to explain herself properly.

Answer: Counterproductive

Explanation: This is extremely unhelpful and contrary to the police expectations. You will only make the woman more upset.

2. Ask the woman to take a seat and you will contact someone who can assist her.

Answer: Fairly Efficient

Explanation: This is a fairly efficient response, as you are still providing the woman with adequate assistance. That being said, you should do your utmost to try and understand the woman's issue, before you contact someone else to assist her.

3. Ask the woman if she could talk a little louder.

Answer: Inefficient

Explanation: This is an inefficient response. The problem is not that the woman is talking too quietly, but with the language barrier.

4. Try to calm the woman down, before speaking to her slowly and clearly, and trying to establish clues from her language.

Answer: Efficient

Explanation: This is the most efficient response to the scenario. You are making a sustained effort to understand the woman's issue yourself, before moving this to someone with more authority.

Q25.

1. Approach the man and attempt to find out his name. Ask around to see if he has any friends in the vicinity.

Answer: Inefficient

Explanation: This is not helpful. The man needs medical attention.

2. Immediately radio for the nearest ambulance, and stay with the man until it arrives.

Answer: Efficient

Explanation: This is the most efficient response. You don't know whether the man is in a fit state to even travel to the ambulance. Therefore, the best course of action is for you to remain with the man, until medical assistance arrives.

3. Try and pick the man up, and escort him to the nearest ambulance.

Answer: Fairly Efficient

Explanation: This is a fairly efficient response, which allows the man to receive immediate medical attention. That being said, it is better to remain with the man until the ambulance arrives, rather than making him take the trip to the ambulance, and risk further harm.

4. Ask the man if he can stand up. If he can't, place him under arrest for being drunk and disorderly.

Answer: Counterproductive

Explanation: This is a counterproductive response. The man is clearly unwell, he needs medical assistance as soon as possible.

Q26.

1. Ask the officer to find someone else to help him, as you are finished work for the day.

Answer: Counterproductive

Explanation: This is counterproductive, because you are a) setting a bad example b) not being helpful. Although your shift has finished, it is good practice to help out the trainee, and sets a good example moving forward.

2. Sit down with the trainee and go through the case report, making sure he's included all of the essential details.

Answer: Efficient

Explanation: This is an efficient response. You are taking the time to ensure that the case report is correct, thereby putting good police work first and foremost.

3. Tell the trainee that you are confident in his ability to file a good case report, and that he should just submit it.

Answer: Inefficient

Explanation: This is an inefficient response. There could be errors in the case report, which need addressing.

4. Take a quick look over the case report, and give the trainee some tips, before heading off for the evening.

Answer: Fairly Efficient

Explanation: This is a fairly efficient response, as you are doing exactly what the trainee has asked you to do. That being said, in this circumstance, there is no reason that you can't go the extra mile.

Q27.

1. Immediately step between the two individuals and try to calm the situation.

Answer: Efficient

Explanation: This is an efficient response to the situation. Your first line of response should be to intervene and prevent things from escalating further.

2. Inform the two individuals that they are acting extremely unprofessionally, and that you will need to report this incident to the head of station.

Answer: Fairly Efficient

Explanation: This is a fairly efficient response, but at the same time, is not completely necessary. Disagreements happen, there is no reason for you to report this to the head of station unless things get really serious.

3. Let the two individuals fight it out. It's character building.

Answer: Counterproductive

Explanation: This is highly counterproductive. Not only would this set a terrible example, but violence is unacceptable.

4. Confront trainee two for his aggression. Threats are totally unacceptable.

Answer: Inefficient

Explanation: This is inefficient. Both parties are to blame, so blaming just one of them will only make things worse.

Q28.

1. 'Please, calm down sir. We are requested to check individuals based on whether we think they look suspicious. In this case, my partner has every right to examine your bag.'

Answer: Counterproductive

Explanation: This is a response which will inflame the situation, and is simply not true!

2. 'You are being extremely aggressive sir. If you don't calm down, we will have to detain you.'

Answer: Inefficient

Explanation: This is an overreaction. You don't need to detain the man, you can just refuse him access to the stadium. A response like this could make him even angrier.

3. 'This is a standard security check, sir. Please calm down so that we can check your bag.'

Answer: Fairly Efficient

Explanation: This is a fairly efficient response, but could still be better. Along with informing the man about the nature of the security checks, you need to make sure that you inform him that it has nothing to do with the colour of his skin.

4. 'Our security checks are conducted at random, sir. It has nothing to do with the colour of your skin.'

Answer: Efficient

Explanation: This is an efficient response. You are clearing informing the man about the security check procedure, and why it is taking place, as well as reassuring him that this is not a racist action.

Q29.

1. 'I'm very sorry about that, Madam. I'll contact the security service and get them on the case.'

Answer: Counterproductive

Explanation: This is a counterproductive response. The policy clearly states that the man (who is blind) is allowed his dog on the premises. Therefore, the woman is in the wrong.

2. 'While it's true that this centre does not allow animals on the premises, we do make an exception for disabled individuals, who would otherwise not be able to attend without these animals. For this reason, I cannot help you with this matter.'

Answer: Efficient

Explanation: This is an efficient response. You are clearly indicating the centre's policy regarding this matter, and explaining to the woman why she is in the wrong.

3. 'Guide dogs are permitted. I believe that you are being quite ignorant in this regard, Madam.'

Answer: Inefficient

Explanation: This is a rude and blunt response, and labelling the woman ignorant will only serve to make her angrier.

4. 'Madam, I'm sure you can understand that guide dogs are essential in some circumstances. For this reason, I cannot help you.'

Answer: Fairly Efficient

Explanation: This is a fairly efficient response, but it could be clearer on the centre's rules and policies.

Q30.

1. Separate the two boys, and then ask them to leave the premises.

Answer: Fairly Efficient

Explanation: This is a fairly efficient response, but asking the two boys to leave the premises might be a step too far. Arguments happen, especially when it comes to sport. As long as the dispute is resolved, there is no reason to kick them out.

2. Wait until the fight is finished, and then warn both boys about their bad behaviour.

Answer: Inefficient

Explanation: This is an inefficient response. You shouldn't wait until the fight is over, you should intervene and stop it right away!

3. Separate the two boys, and warn them that violence is not a way to solve disputes.

Answer: Efficient

Explanation: This is an efficient response. You are clearly laying out the correct approach to the issue, and as a result should ensure that this does not occur again.

4. Arrest both of the boys. Fighting in public is not acceptable.

Answer: Counterproductive

Explanation: This is an overreaction, especially considering they are schoolchildren.

Q31.

1. Knock on the window. If you get no response, call the emergency services.

Answer: Efficient

Explanation: This is an efficient response, as you are taking immediate action. It's better to be safe than sorry.

2. Leave the man to it. He's probably sleeping.

Answer: Inefficient

Explanation: This is an inefficient response. You are simply doing nothing, instead of taking positive action.

3. Smash the car window. The man could be in serious trouble.

Answer: Counterproductive

Explanation: This is a counterproductive response, as it constitutes an overreaction.

4. Knock several times on the window. If you get no response, call police HQ and ask them to check who the car's license plate belongs to.

Answer: Fairly Efficient

Explanation: This is a fairly efficient response, as you are making a sustained attempt to work out the identity of the driver, and whether there is a missing person's alert out for him.

Q32.

1. Ask both men to go with your fellow officer to the station, to give a statement.

Answer: Fairly Efficient

Explanation: This is a fairly efficient response, as you are dealing with the matter in a professional way. That being said, it could be better, as it seems unfair to delay the man in the blue shirt from attending the match – as he has done nothing wrong.

2. Place the man in the red shirt under arrest. Check whether the man in the blue shirt requires medical assistance, before granting him access to the stadium.

Answer: Efficient

Explanation: This is a very efficient response. The man in the blue shirt has not acted violently, unlike the man in the red shirt, who needs to be detained for his behaviour.

3. Arrest both men. Violent behaviour is unacceptable.

Answer: Inefficient

Explanation: This is an inefficient response, as the man in the blue shirt certainly does not deserve to be arrested.

4. Give both men a caution, and then allow them into the stadium, separately.

Answer: Counterproductive

Explanation: This is a counterproductive response. Allowing both men into the stadium could result in more violence.

Q33.

1. Call the station and let them know about the situation. Promise to be in as soon as possible.

Answer: Efficient

Explanation: This is a very efficient response. You are giving the station plenty of notice about the situation, ensuring they can make preparations for your delay.

2. Call your colleague and ask him to cover the start of your shift.

Answer: Inefficient

Explanation: This is an inefficient response. You should simply call the station and let them know that you will be late, rather than asking your colleague to disrupt his own working schedule.

3. Just get into work when you can. It's not your fault if there's traffic.

Answer: Counterproductive

Explanation: This is a counterproductive response. You need to let the station know that you will be late.

4. Call the head of station on his mobile. It's best to let him know as soon as possible.

Answer: Fairly Efficient

Explanation: This is a fairly efficient, if slightly unnecessary, response. It's good that you've taken the initiative to let the head of station know, but really you only need to contact the station desk.

Q34.

1. Punch the man and pin him to the floor. You have a right to defend yourself.

Answer: Counterproductive

Explanation: This is an extremely aggressive response and could serve to make the situation worse. You do not need to punch the man to detain him.

2. Grab the man and place him under arrest. This is totally unacceptable behaviour.

Answer: Efficient

Explanation: This is a very efficient response. You are dealing with the man in an appropriate and suitable manner. He needs to be detained.

3. Walk away from the situation. You don't need to deal with people like this.

Answer: Inefficient

Explanation: This is an inefficient response. The man has acted in a completely unacceptable manner, and needs to be detained.

4. Radio for backup, and warn the man that his actions will have serious consequences.

Answer: Fairly Efficient

Explanation: This is a fairly efficient response, however it's slightly unnecessary. Although the man has acted unacceptably, the question does not signal him out as a serious threat, just someone who could be detained by yourself.

Q35.

1. Ask your colleague if she would feel comfortable finishing the shift on her own.

Answer: Inefficient

Explanation: This is an inefficient response. Your colleague should not need to finish the shift on her own, and you can easily call the station and ask them to send a replacement.

2. Tell your colleague that it's okay, you'll finish the shift.

Answer: Counterproductive

Explanation: There is no point in you continuing under such circumstances, as you are clearly not in a fit state to perform police work. With this in mind, you should not attempt to carry on working.

3. Ask your colleague if it's possible to take a break and sit down for a bit.

Answer: Fairly Efficient

Explanation: This is a fairly efficient response, but you are also slowing your colleague down. If you are that feeling that unwell, it would be wiser to call the station and ask them to send a replacement.

4. Call police HQ and ask them if they are okay for you to finish early.

Answer: Efficient

Explanation: This is the most efficient response to the situation. If necessary, they can then find someone to replace you for the rest of your shift.

Q36.

1. Correct his mistake and pretend it never happened. You haven't got time for him to amend it himself.

Answer: Inefficient

Explanation: This is an inefficient response, because you are not giving the trainee any indication that he made a mistake, and therefore he will fail to learn from this.

2. Highlight the error in, pencil, and then leave the paperwork on his desk, for the next morning. He needs to learn from his mistakes.

Answer: Fairly Efficient

Explanation: You are giving the trainee a chance to learn from his mistake, although it be better to actually talk with him about the error.

3. Correct his mistake but sit down with him in the next morning to talk about the error.

Answer: Efficient

Explanation: This is the most efficient response to the scenario. You are ensuring that the paperwork gets in on time, whilst still showing him the error of his ways.

4. Call him on his mobile to let him know about his error. Inform him that you are extremely disappointed.

Answer: Counterproductive

Explanation: This is not productive. You are going out of your way to scold the trainee, and offering him no constructive feedback.

Q37.

1. Admonish the trainee officers for their unprofessional behaviour. Tell them that this is not acceptable for police officers.

Answer: Fairly Efficient

Explanation: This is a fairly efficient response, depending on how severe you want to be with the trainees. In this response, you are clearly demonstrating the problem with their behaviour.

2. Laugh along with the trainees, but ask them to come away from the car, and stop them from taking pictures of it.

Answer: Efficient

Explanation: This is the most efficient and reasonable response to the scenario. You are taking a firm but fair approach.

3. Call Police HQ, reporting the trainees immediately. Demand that they are removed from the force.

Answer: Counterproductive

Explanation: This is an enormous overreaction, and not something which warrants being removed from the police.

4. Tell the trainees that they need to delete any images they take of the car.

Answer: Inefficient

Explanation: This is an inefficient response. You don't just need to tell them to delete the images, you need to prevent them from taking pictures full stop.

Q38.

1. Refuse to pull over. Tell your partner that this could be a life and death situation, and that he can eat afterwards.

Answer: Efficient

Explanation: This is the most efficient response. Your fellow officer is in serious trouble, so pulling over here would be highly irresponsible.

2. Explain to your partner why this isn't the right course of action. If he persists, pull over and let him out. Then drive to the callout by yourself.

Answer: Fairly Efficient

Explanation: Although this is still a fairly negative response, at the very least you are making your own way to the crime scene, and your partner will need to deal with the consequences of his own actions.

3. Ask your partner whether he can grab you some chips.

Answer: Counterproductive

Explanation: You should not encouraging or going along with this type of behaviour.

4. Radio ahead to ask whether you are urgently needed at the scene, and if it's okay for you to stop for food.

Answer: Inefficient

Explanation: This is an inefficient response, as you shouldn't need to radio ahead for this. The answer is obvious, you have been called to the scene on an urgent basis.

Q39.

1. 'Sorry, my shift begins in 5 minutes, and I need to prepare for it. You'll have to find someone else.'

Answer: Fairly Efficient

Explanation: This is a fairly efficient, although somewhat rude, response.

2. 'I don't drink tea, so you'll have to find someone else to do it.'

Answer: Counterproductive

Explanation: This is rude, and doesn't give a proper explanation for why you can't complete the task.

3. 'That's fine, but I'll be late for my shift. Hopefully that's okay.'

Answer: Inefficient

Explanation: This is an inefficient response. You need to gain the permission of the head of station, as you can't be late for your shift without his/her consent.

4. 'Let me ask the head of station if it's okay for me to go. If so, sure, I'd be happy to.'

Answer: Efficient

Explanation: This is an efficient response. Before you commit to this task, you should certainly check with the head of station first. Being late for your shift could cause serious problems.

Q40.

1. Inform your colleague that he can always talk to you in confidence, but that you will need to report what he has said, out of concern for his safety.

Answer: Efficient

Explanation: This is the most efficient response. You are taking a responsible approach to this scenario, and still making sure that you are taking the best possible course of action for the individual's welfare.

2. Tell your colleague that you'll keep his secret, and that he can always talk to you when he's feeling down.

Answer: Inefficient

Explanation: This response is inefficient. Although it's good that you have shown your colleague that he can trust you, it is your responsibility to report what he has said to someone with a higher level of authority. His welfare could be at risk.

3. Ask your colleague whether there is any way that he can obtain therapy, as suicide is not the answer.

Answer: Fairly Efficient

Explanation: This is a fairly efficient response to this situation, as you are emphasising an alternative solution to the individual, which does not involve him ending his life. That being said, you still need to report this, and should inform him of that.

4. Ask your colleague not to disclose personal information to you. It's none of your business.

Answer: Counterproductive

Explanation: This is a counterproductive and insensitive response, which could make the individual feel worse.

Q41.

1. Sit down with your partner and tell him that you are concerned about his health. Demand that he cuts back on the fast food.

Answer: Inefficient

Explanation: This is a rude and blunt response, which jumps to conclusions. You don't know that he has put on weight due to fast food.

2. Set up a meeting with your partner and the head of station, to discuss your concerns.

Answer: Fairly Efficient

Explanation: This is a fairly efficient response, as it allows both yourself and a member of the senior management team to provide solutions and help your colleague get back into shape.

3. Go straight to the head of station. Your partner has violated the expectations of the police, and needs to be removed at once.

Answer: Counterproductive

Explanation: This is a counterproductive response. It is a major overreaction and shows no attempt to help your colleague.

4. Sit down with your partner and elaborate on your concerns. Ask him whether there is anything you can do to help him.

Answer: Efficient

Explanation: This is an efficient and polite response. You are laying out your concerns in a reasonable manner, and encouraging your partner to improve his health.

Q42.

1. Arrest woman 2 on charges of theft. Take her back to the station for questioning.

Answer: Counterproductive

Explanation: You don't know that this woman is the thief, therefore you have no grounds to arrest her.

2. Confiscate the bag, and tell both women that they will need to come back with you to the station, where you'll analyse the CCTV footage.

Answer: Efficient

Explanation: This is the most efficient response to the scenario. You are defusing the situation, and ensuring that the correct course of action is taken.

3. Tell the two women to take their dispute elsewhere. You don't have time to deal with petty squabbles.

Answer: Inefficient

Explanation: This is an inefficient response. As a police officer, it is your job to deal with situations like this.

4. Confiscate the bag, and take the details of the two women. Tell them that the police will be in touch.

Answer: Fairly Efficient

Explanation: This is a fairly efficient response, as you are dealing with the situation in a responsible manner. That being said, the person whom the bag does actually belong to will now have to wait to get her possession back, which is unfair.

Q43.

1. Inform your colleague that no, you did not give Perkins permission. Take this matter straight to the head of station.

Answer: Inefficient

Explanation: This is an inefficient response. You are jumping to conclusions, without speaking to Perkins first.

2. Ask your colleague whether she is completely sure of what she saw. Then, ask to speak to Perkins alone.

Answer: Fairly Efficient

Explanation: This is a fairly efficient response, as you are dealing with the situation in a fair and reasonable manner.

3. Accuse your colleague of making up stories. Perkins would never do that.

Answer: Counterproductive

Explanation: This is a counterproductive response. You are being extremely rude to your colleague, who is just trying to help you out.

4. Ask your colleague to clarify the exact time at which this incident occurred. Then, check your desk to see if anything is missing.

Answer: Efficient

Explanation: This is the most efficient response to the situation. You are covering all of the necessary bases first, before speaking to Perkins.

Q44.

1. Find colleague 2 and tell him that you overheard the conversation. Demand to know what is going on.

Answer: Fairly Efficient

Explanation: This is a fairly efficient response. You are enquiring with colleague 2 directly, to discover the problem. That being said, it might be better to take a more measured approach, than demanding to know what's happening.

2. Ignore it. It's none of your business.

Answer: Counterproductive

Explanation: This is a counterproductive response. You shouldn't ignore something as serious as this. Threats are not acceptable.

3. Tell your senior manager what you have heard. He is best placed to deal with this.

Answer: Inefficient

Explanation: This is an inefficient response. Although your senior manager needs to be told about this, it's best to talk with colleague 2 first, to get to the bottom of the situation.

4. Locate colleague 2 and tell him that colleague 1's behaviour is unacceptable. Ask him to come with you to the head of station.

Answer: Efficient

Explanation: This is an efficient response. You are going directly to colleague 2, to speak with him about the issue, before taking it to the head of station.

Q45.

1. Tell your partner that as much as the man disgusts you, you cannot break the law yourselves. Call the station and let them know about the situation.

Answer: Efficient

Explanation: This is the most efficient response to the situation. You need to call this in with police HQ, as soon as possible.

2. Tell your partner that you'll be waiting outside in the car. Leave him to it.

Answer: Counterproductive

Explanation: You cannot allow your partner to behave like this, regardless of the killer's actions.

3. Advise your partner that such behaviour would be breaking the law, but that you won't stand in his way.

Answer: Inefficient

Explanation: This is an inefficient response. Although you are advising your partner on the correct procedure, you are not actually enforcing this.

4. Tell your partner that such behaviour would only lower him to the criminal's level. Urge him to think sensibly.

Answer: Fairly Efficient

Explanation: This is a fairly efficient response, and takes a sensible approach to the situation. That being said, you need to call the station immediately.

Q46.

1. Knock on the door and politely ask the homeowner to turn the music down. You don't want to be dealing with a noise complaint.

Answer: Efficient

Explanation: This is the most efficient response to the situation. You are dealing with the situation in a sensible manner, and giving the homeowner a reasonable chance to amend the problem.

2. Ignore it. When someone makes a noise complaint, you'll deal with the situation.

Answer: Inefficient

Explanation: This is an inefficient response. The music is clearly too loud.

3. Bang on the door, and demand that the homeowner lowers the volume of the music.

Answer: Counterproductive

Explanation: This is counterproductive, as you aren't being polite or reasonable. It's entirely possible that the homeowner hasn't realised how loud their music is, so you should ask them politely to turn it down.

4. Knock on the doors of the houses next to the property. Ask the residents if the noise is bothering them.

Answer: Fairly Efficient

Explanation: This is a fairly efficient response, as you are making direct enquiries into whether the other residents of the neighbourhood are being effected by the noise. That being said, the opinions of just the people next door won't necessarily reflect those of everyone in the street, so it's better to just intervene yourself.

Q47.

1. Ask someone more senior than yourself whether they have any idea what he wants to talk to you about.

Answer: Inefficient

Explanation: This is an inefficient response. The matter is between you and the head of station, it's very unlikely that someone else will know anything about it.

2. Go and knock on his office door earlier, just to make sure you haven't done anything wrong.

Answer: Fairly Efficient

Explanation: This is a fairly efficient, whilst slightly unnecessary, response. It's good to ease your anxiety, but at the same time, your head of station has specifically requested to speak to you at the end of the day; not now. You might be disturbing them in the middle of something important.

3. Leave early, so that you don't have to deal with him until tomorrow.

Answer: Counterproductive

Explanation: This is clearly a bad response, and will make the situation worse.

4. Look through your recent case report history, just in case he wants to discuss any of this with you. It's best to be prepared.

Answer: Efficient

Explanation: This is an efficient response, as you are doing your utmost to prepare for whatever the head of station wants to talk about.

Q48.

1. Feign ignorance. There's no need for you to risk your job over something so trivial.

Answer: Counterproductive

Explanation: This is a counterproductive response. You are lying to the head of station, and not taking responsibility.

2. Own up to the mistake, but tell the head of station that somebody else should have made sure the locker was secured.

Answer: Inefficient

Explanation: This is an inefficient response. You are blaming someone else for your error!

3. Apologise for the error and assure the head of station that it won't happen again.

Answer: Fairly Efficient

Explanation: This is a fairly efficient response, as you are owning up to the mistake and giving your head of station an assurance that you've learned from it.

4. Apologise for the error, and ask the head of station for tips on how you can make sure this doesn't happen again.

Answer: Efficient

Explanation: This is a very efficient response. You are owning up to the mistake, and demonstrating your desire to improve for the future.

Q49.

1. Take your colleague to one side and remind him of what the head of station said.

Answer: Counterproductive

Explanation: This is a counterproductive response. It is not enough to simply remind your colleague of station orders. You need to send the journalist away too.

2. Step in and immediately put a halt to the interview. Inform your colleague that he needs to ring police HQ immediately, to inform them of what he's just done.

Answer: Efficient

Explanation: This is an efficient response. It is your colleague's responsibility to inform police HQ of what he's done, and you are ensuring that he does this.

3. Step in and put a stop to the interview. Send the journalist away, before calling police HQ to inform them of the situation.

Answer: Fairly Efficient

Explanation: This is a fairly efficient response. You are making the right decision to call police HQ, but ideally it should be your colleague who does this, admitting to his mistake.

4. Ask the journalist to leave immediately. Tell your colleague that he must not share information with anyone else.

Answer: Inefficient

Explanation: This is an inefficient response. You are not doing enough to fix the problem.

Q50.

1. Inform your colleague that although he might not agree with the woman's views, there are no grounds to arrest her.

Answer: Efficient

Explanation: This is the most efficient response to the situation. You are addressing the problem in a calm and sensible manner, in a way that is in line with the police expectations.

2. Inform your colleague that it's important to be respectful of everybody's views, regardless of whether he agrees with them. Place the woman under arrest.

Answer: Counterproductive

Explanation: You can't place the woman under arrest for this.

3. Tell your colleague that he needs to be more accepting of alternative viewpoints. Encourage him to go and speak to the woman about her tattoo.

Answer: Inefficient

Explanation: There is no reason for the man to go and speak to the woman about her tattoo. Provided she is not committing an offence, he should ignore her.

4. Ignore your colleague. He's entitled to his own views, but you won't be placing anyone under arrest.

Answer: Fairly Efficient

Explanation: This is fairly efficient, but you still need to remind your colleague about the police expectations.

Suggested Answers: Test 2

Q1.

1. Say no. You are already settled in at your desk and to move would cause unnecessary upheaval.

Answer: Counterproductive

Explanation: This is counterproductive. The lady is disabled and by not agreeing to her request you are failing to help improve her working environment. By choosing this option you will also serve to deteriorate your working relationship with both her and the rest of your team.

2. Say yes. This is not a problem for you and you can see why moving desks would help her out and improve her working day.

Answer: Efficient

Explanation: This is efficient. Not only does it improve her working environment, it also serves to improve/enhance relations within the office environment.

3. Tell her to speak to your boss first, to see if he is in agreement with her request. If he doesn't have a problem with it, neither do you.

Answer: Fairly Efficient

Explanation: This is fairly efficient, simply because you are informing your boss what the proposed plan is regarding swapping desks.

4. Tell her you would be willing to swap desks providing she is prepared to move all of your belongings to the new desk.

Answer: Inefficient

Explanation: This is inefficient. Although you have agreed to the desk swap, the lady is in a wheelchair and may not be capable of moving all of your office belongings.

Q2.

1. Consult with the other people in the carriage as to what to do.

Answer: Inefficient

Explanation: This is unprofessional. It's nothing to do with the other people in the carriage, and they shouldn't have to tell you how to do your job.

2. Allow him to pay the full ticket fare to his intended stop.

Answer: Fairly Efficient

Explanation: This is fairly efficient, in the sense that you are showing compassion and common sense. However, technically the man is breaking the law by travelling without buying a ticket first. It could be argued that you should fine him. If everyone made this excuse and bought their tickets on the train instead, train operating companies could lose hundreds of thousands of pounds. There is also no way to ascertain whether he is lying about what stop he boarded at.

3. Perform a citizen's arrest. This man is a criminal.

Answer: Counterproductive

Explanation: This is counterproductive. The man has done nothing to warrant a citizen's arrest, and certainly does not appear to be dangerous or in need of restraint.

4. Issue the man with a standard penalty fare.

Answer: Efficient

Explanation: Regardless of his personal circumstances, the man has broken the rules, and therefore you need to issue him with a penalty fare.

Q3.

1. Take the new employee to one side and tell him that his behaviour needs to change.

Answer: Fairly Efficient

Explanation: This is a fairly efficient response. You are taking steps to try and amend the situation, without going to management straight away. By discussing it with the new employee to one side, you are not humiliating them in front of your other colleagues.

2. Go to your manager and explain the situation.

Answer: Inefficient

Explanation: This is an inefficient response, as the woman has already said that she does not want to jeopardise the employee's position at the company. Therefore it is not up to you to go to management.

3. Encourage your female colleagues to speak to your manager.

Answer: Efficient

Explanation: This is efficient, as it is the right thing to do. Although you should of course take some responsibility for helping your colleagues, ultimately it is their issue to take to the manager

4. Ignore the behaviour. He's only joking.

Answer: Counterproductive

Explanation: This is counterproductive. Sexual harassment/inappropriateness is a serious issue.

Q4.

1. Agree to act as a witness, but tell the chairman that there is no evidence to suggest sexism.

Answer: Efficient

Explanation: This is efficient, as it is an honest response. If you have not seen any evidence of sexism, then you cannot support these claims. All you need to do is tell the chairman what you saw.

2. Tell the chairman that you believe your sales manager was acting in a sexist manner.

Answer: Inefficient

Explanation: This is inefficient. As the passage states, you have seen no evidence of sexism.

3. Agree to act a witness. Suggest to the chairman that the department needs some extra help.

Answer: Fairly Efficient

Explanation: This is a fairly efficient response, as you are agreeing to act as a witness, and offering some advice on how to fix other difficult issues. That being said, you haven't been brought into the meeting to discuss the latter.

4. Encourage your colleague to sue the company. Sexism is unacceptable.

Answer: Counterproductive

Explanation: This is counterproductive. Not only have you seen no evidence of sexism, but suing the company would be a fairly extreme course of action.

Q5.

1. Agree to cross over and get an autograph. This could be your only chance to meet such a prestigious author.

Answer: Counterproductive

Explanation: This is counterproductive. It would be extremely unprofessional to abandon your post just to go and get an autograph. Furthermore, the celebrity might not want to be harassed.

2. Tell your colleague that you won't be going anywhere. What they do is up to them.

Answer: Fairly Efficient

Explanation: This demonstrates that you are following the rules and standards expected of you. You are not the keeper of your other colleague, so you cannot force them to stay.

3. Refuse to go, and encourage your colleague to do the same. This would be unprofessional.

Answer: Efficient

Explanation: This is efficient. It would be extremely unprofessional to abandon your post just to go and get an autograph. Furthermore, the person might not want to be harassed. The fact that you have encouraged your colleague to do the same shows that you are thinking in the best interests of the company.

4. Take mobile pictures of the celebrity from afar, but don't approach them.

Answer: Inefficient

Explanation: This is an inefficient response. Although you aren't leaving your post, you are acting unprofessionally.

Q6.

1. Offer to take the man's contact details, so that he can be reimbursed for the price of some of his shopping.

Answer: Inefficient

Explanation: This is inefficient. The man does not need to be reimbursed for his shopping, he just wants his bag back.

2. Tell the man there is nothing that can be done. You snooze, you lose.

Answer: Counterproductive

Explanation: This is counterproductive. You are being extremely unsympathetic and unprofessional, along with refusing to take any responsibility.

3. Report the incident to senior management. Tell the man that your company will be in touch.

Answer: Fairly Efficient

Explanation: This is fairly efficient, as it demonstrates that you are taking reasonable action in order to resolve the issue. Whilst you have been quite vague in terms of getting in contact with him, it still shows that you are acting upon it by going to management.

4. Take the man into a private room where you can write up a report of the incident, which will then be passed on to the police.

Answer: Efficient

Explanation: This is efficient, as it means that you have taken initiative, acted in a responsible manner and then passed the matter over to the organisation best equipped to deal with it. Along with this, you have made the man feel reassured that the case is in good hands.

Q7.

1. Ignore the situation. It's none of your business.

Answer: Efficient

Explanation: This is an efficient response. Customer personal matters are nothing to do with staff, provided they aren't breaking laws or rules.

2. Confront the man on the spot. Cheating is immoral.

Answer: Counterproductive

Explanation: This is a counterproductive response. Regardless of how you feel about the man's behaviour, it's none of your business.

3. Take the man to one side and quietly ask him to explain his behaviour.

Answer: Inefficient

Explanation: This is an inefficient response. Once again, it is none of your business, and you would be acting unprofessionally.

4. Talk to your colleague about your concern, this is a good outlet.

Answer: Fairly Efficient

Explanation: This is a fairly efficient response, as it allows you to discuss the issue without it having an impact on the business.

Q8.

1. 'Pack your bags. You're sacked.'

Answer: Counterproductive

Explanation: Sacking the employee on the spot won't solve anything, and would be unprofessional.

2. 'Mistakes happen. Let's pull the team together and brainstorm some ideas as to how we can fix this.'

Answer: Efficient

Explanation: This is efficient as it allows you to try and reach a positive solution to the situation, whilst gaining suggestions from a wide variety of people.

3. 'Maybe you should consider whether this is the right position for you.'

Answer: Inefficient

Explanation: This is an inefficient response. There will be time to discuss this after the incident has been resolved. All this will do is damage the employee's confidence, making him less likely to successfully complete future tasks.

4. 'Okay, obviously this isn't ideal, but let's think of some solutions. We'll have a serious chat about this at the end of the day though.'

Answer: Fairly Efficient

Explanation: This is a fairly efficient response. You are treating the issue in a constructive manner, but still ensuring that the employee knows that it's a serious mistake.

Q9.

1. 'Hi. I'm really sorry about the incident that occurred yesterday. We hope to see you back at work soon.'

Answer: Fairly Efficient

Explanation: This is fairly efficient, because it shows a willingness to take responsibility for the incident and a level of care for the employee. However, you have failed to make reassurances that the incident is being looked into.

2. 'Hi. Unfortunately, since you are part time, and can no longer work, we are going to have to terminate your contract.'

Answer: Counterproductive

Explanation: This is counterproductive. It shows a lack of care and professionalism, and is completely unfair on the employee, particularly since it was the company's fault to begin with.

3. 'Hi. Do you think you could come in and work on crutches?'

Answer: Inefficient

Explanation: This is inefficient. The employee is obviously unable to continue working on crutches and therefore would not benefit them or the company.

4. 'Hi. I'm really sorry about the incident that took place at work yesterday. I'd like to assure you that we will conduct a full investigation of the incident, to ensure it doesn't happen again.'

Answer: Efficient

Explanation: This is an efficient response to the situation. You are making clear reassurances that the problem will be looked into, and apologising to the employee.

Q10.

1. Spread bad rumours about your manager. Two can play that game.

Answer: Counterproductive

Explanation: This is counterproductive. It is extremely unprofessional, and could only lead to more trouble. You should be the better person.

2. Take your manager to one side and question her on whether the claims are true. Explain why you needed the time off.

Answer: Efficient

Explanation: This is efficient, as it constitutes the most reasonable response. It shows both professionalism and integrity.

3. Arrange a team meeting to try to get to the bottom of this.

Answer: Inefficient

Explanation: This is an inefficient response, as you are involving your colleagues in a situation between you and your manager. You should be aiming to stop them gossiping or getting involved, therefore conducting a meeting will only make the situation worse.

4. Ring your manager in your own time to try and discuss the situation further.

Answer: Fairly Efficient

Explanation: This is a fairly efficient response, as it shows that you are looking to try and resolve the situation in a positive manner.

Q11.

1. Apologise to the customer and say you are sorry but there is nothing more you can do.

Answer: Counterproductive

Explanation: This is counterproductive. Although you are apologising, you are doing nothing to resolve the issue, or rectify the mistake made by the shop.

2. Apologise to the customer and inform her that there is another toy shop 15 miles away in the next town. If she travels there, they might have the toy she wants in stock.

Answer: Fairly efficient

Explanation: This is fairly efficient. Although it is unfortunate that the woman will need to travel so far, you are clearly explaining where she can go to obtain the toy.

3. Apologise unreservedly for the toy not being in stock. Tell her that you will order the toy immediately from your supplier and then deliver it to her home as soon as it arrives. She will not be charged for either the toy or the delivery due to the inconvenience and stress caused.

Answer: Inefficient

Explanation: This is inefficient. Although you are being helpful and polite, the woman still needs to pay for the toy. Giving it to her for free is not the right response, since your company have not done anything wrong.

4. Apologise unreservedly for the toy not being in stock. Tell her that you will order the toy immediately from your supplier and then deliver it to her home as soon as it arrives. She will be charged for the toy, but not for the delivery, due to the inconvenience and stress caused.

Answer: Efficient

Explanation: This is efficient, as you are ordering the toy for her and delivering it direct to her. Although she has to pay for the toy you have agreed to deliver it for free, to compensate for the wasted journey. This will hopefully avoid any ill-feeling on the customer's part and will go part-way to making good the mistake made by the shop.

Q12.

1. Thank them for the money, put it in your pocket, and leave a happy person. Nobody will ever know that you took the money, so there's no harm.

Answer: Counterproductive

Explanation: This is counterproductive. You are in breach of the company's strict policies regarding tips and financial rewards, and you could be dismissed or disciplined for breaking this.

2. Thank them for the money, but explain that you are unable to accept tips or financial rewards of this nature. Tell them that if they would like to give a reward, the supermarket supports local charities and they will be able to donate via their website.

Answer: Efficient

Explanation: This is efficient, as you are politely refusing the generous offer, whilst not placing yourself in danger of being in breach of the company's strict policies regarding tips and financial rewards. Yet you are still giving the customer the option to donate to the supermarkets chosen charity.

3. Thank them for their kind offer, but explain that you are unable to accept tips or financial rewards of this nature.

Answer: Fairly Efficient

Explanation: This is fairly efficient, as you are politely refusing the generous offer whilst not placing yourself in danger of being in breach of the company's strict policies, regarding tips and financial rewards.

4. Walk away and ignore them.

Answer: Inefficient

Explanation: This is inefficient. Whilst you are not placing yourself in danger of being in breach of the company's strict policies regarding tips and financial rewards, the way in which you are handling the situation is rude, and will leave the customer feeling devalued and upset.

Q13.

1. Ignore it. You are at the premise to talk to the staff about a specific subject and it would be inappropriate to say anything there and then.

Answer: Counterproductive

Explanation: This is counterproductive. As a Health and Safety assessor, you have a responsibility to take action.

2. Remove the wedges yourself and then report the situation to the local Fire Safety Officer when you return to your office later that day. He/she can then carry out a formal inspection.

Answer: Fairly Efficient

Explanation: This is a fairly efficient response. Not only are you making the premise safer by removing the wedges whilst you are there, making the premise safer in the process, but you are also informing the Fire Service so they can carry out a thorough inspection of the premise.

3. Inform the responsible person at the warehouse that the wedges need to be moved immediately. Then, once you return to the office you will report the matter to your local Fire Safety Officer so that he/she can carry out a thorough inspection of the premise.

Answer: Efficient

Explanation: This is efficient. Not only are you asking the responsible person to remove the wedges straight away, which educates them and makes the premise safer, you are also informing the Fire Service so they can carry out a thorough inspection of the premise.

4. Remove the wedges holding the doors open yourself and say nothing more about it.

Answer: Inefficient

Explanation: Whilst you are making the premise safer by removing the wedges yourself, it is likely they will be put back soon after. You need to discuss this with someone.

Q14.

1. Join in with the objections. Why change things when everything is going OK as it is?

Answer: Counterproductive

Explanation: Not only are you objecting to the change just because everyone else is, you are also not being open to the opportunities that can be brought to the organisation. For an organisation to grow and develop, change is inevitable.

2. Keep your head down. Whilst you don't agree with the changes you don't want to get into trouble for raising your concerns.

Answer: Inefficient

Explanation: This isn't particularly efficient. You are 'sort of' accepting the changes, despite disagreeing with them. In order for changes to be successful in any organisation, everyone must believe in them.

3. Accept the changes yourself. It doesn't matter what the others think. After all, they are entitled to their own opinion.

Answer: Fairly Efficient

Explanation: This is a fairly efficient response. Whilst you are not going the extra mile to educate your work colleagues on the benefit of change, you are accepting of them.

4. Accept and embrace the changes. Change is part of working life. You would also try and explain the benefit of the changes to those who are sceptical.

Answer: Efficient

Explanation: Not only are you embracing and accepting the changes, but you are also going out of your way to explain the benefit to others, which in turn improves the efficiency of the organisation.

Q15.

1. Carry out the task as requested, professionally, even though it will mean that you have to stay behind at work for an additional 10 minutes.

Answer: Efficient

Explanation: This is efficient, as you are willing to stay behind and do the job to the standard required, something which will be appreciated by your line manager.

2. Inform your manager that you are happy to complete the task, but ask if you can finish slightly earlier tomorrow to compensate.

Answer: Fairly Efficient

Explanation: This is a fairly efficient response, as you are completing the task, but still explaining the situation to your manager.

3. Carry out the task to a slightly lesser standard, therefore finishing your shift on time.

Answer: Inefficient

Explanation: This is an inefficient response. Although you are agreeing to do the task, you are not carrying it out to the required standard.

4. Politely refuse to carry out the task.

Answer: Counterproductive

Explanation: This is counterproductive, as the task will not get done, and the workplace will be left untidy for the oncoming shift.

Q16.

1. Get the team together and tell them that, if matters do not improve, you will speak to the main boss about getting them replaced.

Answer: Counterproductive

Explanation: This is counterproductive. Not only could this have a negative impact on team morale, you are also failing to establish why the mistakes are being made in the first place. If you dismiss the team and replace them with new staff, the same mistakes might not go away.

2. Hold a team meeting as soon as possible to establish the reasons why so many mistakes are being made. Then, formulate and agree a plan with all of the team in order to improve performance.

Answer: Efficient

Explanation: This is efficient, as you are communicating with the team to establish why the mistakes are being made. This will enable you to create a plan to improve performance that everyone can follow.

3. Get stuck in yourself more to help the team out. Clearly they are very busy and they could do with an extra pair of hands.

Answer: Inefficient

Explanation: This is inefficient, because the team will see that you are failing to tackle the reason why mistakes are being made. As their manager, you are responsible for managing them, not doing their job for them.

4. Speak to your boss and explain to her that you need to take on another member of staff to ease the pressure on the team.

Answer: Fairly Efficient

Explanation: This is fairly efficient. If the mistakes are being made due to increased workload, it seems logical to employ another member of staff during this busy annual peak.

Q17.

1. Walk around the contents and go for my tea break. You are legally entitled to a break and someone else will be able to clear up the mess.

Answer: Counterproductive

Explanation: This is counterproductive. Whilst you are entitled to your tea break, you are doing nothing about the issue. At the very least you should inform your manager so that someone else can start tidying up the mess.

2. Inform your manager that you are going to put the contents back on the shelf and request that you take your 10-minute tea break after the job is complete.

Answer: Efficient

Explanation: This is an efficient response. Not only are you taking immediate action by putting the contents back on the shelf, but you are also ensuring that you get your tea break.

3. Inform your manager that the contents have fallen on the floor, and ask him if he can find someone else to put the contents back on the shelf, as you are about to go on your tea break.

Answer: Inefficient

Explanation: This is inefficient. Although you are informing your manager about the problem, everybody is really busy serving customers, and they will not be able to put the contents back on the shelf.

4. Forget about your tea break and put the contents back on the shelf yourself.

Answer: Fairly Efficient

Explanation: This is a fairly efficient response, as you are dealing with the problem. That being said, you still need to find the time to take your break. If you don't do this, then you will tire faster during the rest of the day, and you may not perform to the best of your ability.

Q18.

1. Apologise to the people in the queue and inform them you will not be able to serve them due to the breakdown of the coffee machine, which is beyond your control. Then, close the shop and make your way home.

Answer: Counterproductive

Explanation: This is a counterproductive response. Whilst you are apologising to the customers, you are not offering them an alternative drink. You are simply giving up and going home.

2. Apologise to the people in the queue and inform them that you will only be able to serve soft drinks and tea due to the breakdown of the coffee machine. Then, create a sign that says 'COFFEE MACHINE BROKEN – WE ARE ONLY ABLE TO SERVE SOFT DRINKS AND TEA – APOLOGIES FOR ANY INCONVENIENCE CAUSED' and place it on the shop door front so that people can make a decision whether or not they want to come in.

Answer: Efficient

Explanation: This is efficient. Not only are you apologising to the customers, you are also offering people an alternative drink and you are also informing people of the issue before they enter the shop. This will save you considerable time having to explain to everyone who comes into the shop of the issue.

3. Apologise to each person as they reach the front of the queue and explain to them that you are unable to serve coffee but that you can serve them soft drinks or tea.

Answer: Fairly Efficient

Explanation: Although you will need to repeat yourself each time someone comes into the shop, you are still keeping the shop open and offering alternative drinks.

4. Call your boss and ask her what she wants you to do.

Answer: Inefficient

Explanation: This an inefficient response. Yes, you are doing something about the problem, but you are not working on your own initiative. You don't need to call your boss about this.

Q19.

1. Tell him you are not obliged to go into reasons why he was not successful, and ask him to leave.

Answer: Counterproductive

Explanation: This is a counterproductive response. Whilst you are correct in the fact that you are not obliged to go into the reasons why he was unsuccessful, this does not present your company in a positive light. It would just serve to make the situation worse.

2. Provide him with a short list of reasons for why he was unsuccessful, and encourage him to apply for future positions.

Answer: Fairly Efficient

Explanation: This is a fairly efficient response. You are potentially leading him along and giving him false hope. He will, quite rightly, expect to be successful at any future interviews he attends. This option just places you in a difficult position.

3. Listen to his concerns and allow him to vent his frustrations. Once he has finished, explain to him that there is a robust and thorough selection process in place and that unfortunately, on this occasion, he was unsuccessful and that someone else was found more suitable for the role. Then, offer him constructive feedback on his performance during the interview.

Answer: Efficient

Explanation: This is an efficient response. You are allowing him to get his frustrations off his chest, and you are giving him a valid reason for why he was unsuccessful. You are then offering him feedback on his performance so that he can improve for any future interviews he might attend.

4. Invite him to sit down and make him a cup of tea. Whilst you are out of the office, call your boss and ask for advice on how to deal with the situation.

Answer: Inefficient

Explanation: This is an inefficient response. Although you are seeking advice on what to do next from your manager, you are not taking the lead and using your initiative to deal with the situation, something which would be expected from a supervisor.

Q20.

1. Apologise for the inconvenience that has been caused through the defective shaver. Explain to the customer the company's refund policy and that a receipt is required for a refund or exchange. However, explain to him that, if he can provide proof of purchase, by way of a card statement, that you will ask your manager if you can exchange the shaver for him.

Answer: Efficient

Explanation: This is efficient. Although a receipt is required for exchange or refund, you are using your initiative and trying to find an alternative solution to rectify the problem.

2. Explain to him that, because he does not have a receipt, you are not able to help him.

Answer: Counterproductive

Explanation: This is counterproductive. Although you are correct in the fact that he needs a receipt in order to exchange the defective shaver, you are doing nothing at all to solve the problem.

3. Apologise for the inconvenience that has been caused through the defective shaver and then happily exchange the defective shaver for a new one.

Answer: Inefficient

Explanation: This is inefficient. You cannot exchange the shaver until you have proof that it has been purchased from your store.

4. Ask your manager what he thinks you should do.

Answer: Fairly Efficient

Explanation: This is fairly efficient. Due to your position as a retail assistant, it is good practice to ask your manager for advice.

Q21.

1. As soon as there becomes a natural break in her talk, raise your hand and explain that you are finding it difficult to understand most of what she is saying. Respectfully ask if she would please slow down so that you can take in all of the important information she is relaying.

Answer: Efficient

Explanation: This is efficient, as it is important that you understand what is being said at the meeting. If you wait until the end, your manager will have to go through the entire meeting again.

2. Wait until the end of the meeting and then ask your work colleagues for clarification on what she was saying.

Answer: Fairly Efficient

Explanation: This is fairly efficient, as you are seeking help from your other colleagues.

3. Wait to the end of the meeting before speaking to her in private and explain to her that you didn't understand most of what she was saying.

Answer: Inefficient

Explanation: This is inefficient. Yes, you will get to hear everything that was said at the meeting; however, your manager will have to repeat all of the meeting points again, which will take considerable time.

4. Do nothing

Answer: Counterproductive

Explanation: This is counterproductive, as you will never get to understand what was said during the meeting.

Q22.

1. Challenge her in a respectable manner and say that you think she is wrong for saying these things about a senior member of the team.

Answer: Fairly Efficient

Explanation: This is fairly efficient, as you are standing your ground and being firm about how you feel other members of the organisation are treated.

2. Thank her for the information and be on your guard from now on when dealing with my manager.

Answer: Inefficient

Explanation: This is inefficient. Whilst it may appear to be a good thing that you have taken on-board her comments, it is not a good thing to pre-judge people based on the comments or viewpoints of just one person.

3. Thank her for the information but explain that you do not want to pre-judge people and you want to have an entirely open mind. You will take him as you find him.

Answer: Efficient

Explanation: This is efficient, as it shows that you are not prepared to pre-judge people. After all, she may have a personal grudge against the manager and be deliberately trying to cause him harm.

4. Thank her for the information and then ask other people within the organisation if they have had the same experience whilst working with your manager.

Answer: Counterproductive.

Explanation: You could end up discussing what you have heard with a member of the team who is close/supportive of the manager, and the gossip could get back to him, which might not be good for your future prospects.

Q23.

1. Explain that you cannot meet their request as you have lots of paperwork work to catch up on.

Answer: Counterproductive

Explanation: This is counterproductive, as it does nothing to help out the head office.

2. Explain to head office that you have lots of paperwork to catch up on and ask them how they want you to prioritise your work.

Answer: Inefficient

Explanation: This is inefficient. You are a manager and you should be able to work out how to prioritise your own workload. This shows a lack of professionalism and initiative.

3. Tell head office that you have lots of paperwork to catch up on but that you are prepared to ring around the other hotels in the region to see if there is another manager available to go to the hotel. If not, then you would be prepared to go and you would have to catch up with your paperwork another time.

Answer: Fairly Efficient

Explanation: This is fairly efficient, as you are offering to ring around to find another manager to cover. Failing that, you are still happy to take up the task.

4. Agree to go to the hotel for the rest of the day and take your paperwork with you to do, whilst you are there.

Answer: Efficient

Explanation: This is efficient, as you are agreeing to go to the hotel and you will work on your paperwork whilst you are there.

Q24.

1. Speak to your colleague in private and ask him whether anything is wrong. You would also offer your support to see if you can help him through this difficult period he is going through.

Answer: Efficient

Explanation: This is efficient, as you are asking your colleague if there is anything wrong. Your colleague is likely to feel supported. This would be the best way to handle this type of situation.

2. Approach your manager in confidence and tell him that you think there might be something wrong with your work colleague that is having an impact on his work performance.

Answer: Fairly Efficient

Explanation: This is fairly efficient, as you are raising your concerns with your manager and making him aware that there may be something more going on than first meets the eye. It is not efficient, as it's not really your place to get involved.

3. Do nothing. You do not want to interfere as it is not your problem.

Answer: Counterproductive

Explanation: This is counterproductive. You are aware there is an issue, yet you are choosing to do nothing about it.

4. Speak to your work colleague and offer to do some of his work for him in order to ease the pressure he is under from his manager.

Answer: Inefficient

Explanation: This an inefficient response, as it does nothing to resolve the poor performance your colleague has been reprimanded for.

Q25.

1. Tell the oncoming shift workers that they will have to work on their own, unsupervised, for 30 minutes until their supervisor arrives.

Answer: Inefficient

Explanation: This is inefficient. Teamwork is important, and you should be prepared to wait for the oncoming shift supervisor.

2. Call your girlfriend and tell her you will be late coming home. Then, supervise the oncoming shift workers until their supervisor arrives.

Answer: Efficient

Explanation: This is efficient, and constitutes what would be expected of a supervisor in this type of role.

3. Call your boss and ask her what she thinks you should do.

Answer: Fairly Efficient

Explanation: This is fairly efficient. That being said, your boss is likely to ask if you will wait for the oncoming supervisor to arrive anyway, so you may as well stay on and wait for him.

4. Just leave at the end of your shift. The fact that he is going to be late is not your problem.

Answer: Counterproductive

Explanation: This is a counterproductive response, as you are not even informing the oncoming shift workers that their supervisor will be late.

Q26.

1. Complete the 6-month supervision period as planned and don't say anything about how you feel.

Answer: Inefficient

Explanation: This is inefficient, as it is important to speak to your manager about your frustrations

2. Tell your work colleagues how you feel and get their advice on what they think you should do.

Answer: Fairly Efficient

Explanation: This is a fairly efficient response. However, remember that whilst there is nothing wrong with speaking to your work colleagues, they are not the ones in the position to make a change to your supervised working.

3. Start working more on your own without telling anyone.

Answer: Counterproductive

Explanation: This is counterproductive. Your line manager would be extremely disappointed if you started working unsupervised, against his instructions. This could also lead to discipline procedures against you.

4. Arrange a meeting with your line manager to explain how you now feel ready to work more on your own, unsupervised. Ask his permission for the supervision period to come to an end.

Answer: Efficient

Explanation: This is efficient, as you are discussing how you feel with your line manager. He can then make the decision on whether or not to reduce the time period that you are supervised.

Q27.

1. Spend time with the team member to identify ways in which she can manage her time efficiently so that she can attend the team development meeting.

Answer: Efficient

Explanation: This is efficient, as you are showing support to the team member, and you are also identifying ways to manage her time.

2. Tell the team member that the team development meeting is mandatory. She must attend.

Answer: Inefficient

Explanation: This is inefficient, as it will only add stress to how she is feeling. It is not the most professional way to handle the situation.

3. Tell the team member that you understand how she is feeling and that she does not need to attend the team development meeting.

Answer: Counterproductive

Explanation: This is counterproductive, as you are failing to tackle the reasons why she is unable to cope with the increased workload. She is then more likely not to attend future meetings if she feels you give her permission not to attend. This also demonstrates to the other team members that it is OK to skip team meetings.

4. Get a member of staff from another team to cover the team member's workload during the day of the meeting so that she can attend.

Answer: Fairly Efficient

Explanation: This is fairly efficient, as it allows the team member to attend the team development meeting whilst her work is getting done.

Q28.

1. You tell your colleague that he is being extremely unprofessional and tell him to arrange a lift home and sober up.

Answer: Efficient

Explanation: This is efficient. It is important that everyone remains safe, and an employee who is drunk could cause hazards. The employee needs to sober up before he can resume working.

2. You inform your colleague that you are aware of the said issue, and encourage him to seek help.

Answer: Fairly Efficient

Explanation: This is fairly efficient, as you are encouraging the man to get the right support.

3. You get another one of your colleagues to drive him home, so you can continue working in peace.

Answer: Inefficient

Explanation: This is inefficient. Getting another colleague to drive him home will cause further disruption to the workplace, and therefore is causing more disorder.

4. You tell him to make a cup of coffee and sober up, and get on with his work quietly.

Answer: Counterproductive

Explanation: This is counterproductive. An employee who is drunk is not going to perform their duties to the best of their ability, and therefore this will compromise their work.

Q29.

1. Explain to your team member that the group need her, and that she should rise above it and continue with the project.

Answer: Inefficient

Explanation: This is inefficient. Even though it will boost your team member's confidence, this does not deal with the current situation.

2. Wait to see if you hear anything as mentioned by the individual, and then take action.

Answer: Counterproductive

Explanation: This is counterproductive. Waiting to see if anything happens is not dealing with the current situation. It shows that you do not believe your team member, and shows a lack of initiative at handling difficult situations.

3. Sit the individual in question down, and ask their side of the story.

Answer: Fairly Efficient

Explanation: This option is fairly efficient. Sitting the individual in question down, and asking their side of the story shows that you are working towards resolving the issue by gaining a full understanding of what is happening.

4. Sit them both down to try and resolve the issue, before continuing on with the project.

Answer: Efficient

Explanation: This is efficient. Sitting both team members down, and discussing how to resolve the situation, not only shows professionalism, but it also handles the situation in a mature and efficient manner.

Q30.

1. Explain to your boss that the presentation is being presented that afternoon, and ask him for ideas on how to implement this information in time.

Answer: Fairly Efficient

Explanation: This is a fairly efficient response. You are clearly explaining the situation to your boss, and asking him for advice.

2. Inform your boss that whilst you cannot add in this information due to time constraints, you will be happy to answer any questions they have.

Answer: Inefficient

Explanation: While inviting people in to ask questions at the end of the interview, this will not demonstrate all of the important information that has been missed in the presentation. This doesn't fix your presentation, and will suggest that you ran out of time to complete it

3. Ignore your boss's concerns and present the presentation the way it is.

Answer: Counterproductive

Explanation: Ignoring your boss's comments regarding the presentation does not fix the issues, nor does it deal with the situation.

4. Ask your colleagues to help you with the additional information, so that you can ensure the work gets added.

Answer: Efficient

Explanation: This is an efficient response. Asking for help from your colleagues will allow you to get the extra information added in time for the presentation. It shows that you are willing to take help from other people, and will therefore be able to complete the presentation to a better standard.

Online Assessment Centre

IMPORTANT: If you take a SJT before you are invited to participate in the Online Assessment Process, you will almost certainly not need to take the new SJT format and instead you will skip straight to Stage 2 of the new Online Assessment Process.

This chapter outlines the new College of Policing Online Assessment Process, which is set to be used nationally by England and Wales police forces throughout 2020. It is likely this online assessment process will be in place for all police constable applicants due to the COVID-19 pandemic, but please check with your own constabulary to confirm.

Within this the following chapters, we will look at what the new assessment will involve, the timeline for completion, how candidates will be assessed, how candidates can prepare, and some frequently asked questions on this brand-new police selection process.

WHO IS THE COLLEGE OF POLICING ONLINE ASSESSMENT PROCESS FOR?

The new online assessment process has been put together by the College of Policing as an assessment tool for police forces to use in the recruitment process of police constables/police officers.

HOW IS THE POLICE ONLINE ASSESSMENT STRUCTURED?

The new police online assessment process can be broken down into four core exercises:

1. Situational Judgement Test (SJT)

2. Video Interview (competency-based)

3. Written Exercise

4. Briefing/Presentation Exercise

These exercises test the same competencies and values that are used in policing. As a candidate, you will be expected to demonstrate these competencies and values throughout these exercises.

WHAT COMPETENCIES ARE ASSESSED?

The competencies and values used in the new online police assessment centre are the same beliefs and behaviours expected of all those policing.

These include the six core competencies:

- Emotionally aware
- Innovative & open-minded
- Analyse critically
- Deliver, support, & inspire
- Collaborative
- Take ownership

And the four core values:

- Transparency
- Integrity
- Public service
- Impartiality

Police Values

The police values are a key part of the basic behavioural guidelines for any police employee. As one of the most esteemed and respected organisations in the world, the UK Police naturally have a number of values that they expect all candidates and employees to abide by, along with a strong code of ethics. In the past, the police have largely focused on the competencies of candidates rather than on their values as a person. While these values were still important, they played a secondary role. Now, the police are recognising that it's extremely important to hire candidates with strong values and ethics,. The new police values are as follows:

Impartiality

Impartiality is all about staying true to the key principles of fairness and objectivity. It's absolutely vital that police constables can be impartial when dealing with members of the public, and with their colleagues. You must treat every single person that you meet with fairness and equal consideration, and be able to recognise and reprimand any and all forms of discrimination. Police constables must be able to put aside their personal feelings or beliefs and make decisions with clear logic and rationale.

A police constable who can act with impartiality can:

- Understand the varying needs of individuals, and take these into account when making decisions.

- Treat every person in a fair and respectful manner.

- Ensure that they communicate effectively with everyone they meet, clearly relaying the message.

- Challenge prejudice and discrimination, whenever it arises.

- Make decisions using fair and objective reasoning.

- Value and appreciate the opinions of everyone whom they come into contact with, provided they are not in contradiction with the police code of ethics.

Integrity

Integrity is another extremely important part of the police code of ethics. Police constables must be able to act with integrity and decency at all times, and be capable of recognising both good and poor performance. As a police constable, your professionalism is absolutely integral. You are a representative of the police – a role model – and therefore it's fundamental that you can present an honest and trustworthy approach to the public. By doing this, you can build confidence with the public in the police force and deliver a far more effective service.

A police constable with integrity can:

- Ensure that they behave in accordance with the police code of ethics, and make decisions that are focused on benefitting the public.

- Make decisions that will improve the reputation of the police, and understand their position as a role model within society.

- Welcome and take on board constructive criticism.

- Use their position of authority in society in a fair and professional manner, and as a force for positive change.

Public Service

The third value on the list is public service. This value again links back to the police code of ethics, and is essentially about acting with the best interests of the public in mind. The police are there to protect the public, and safeguard them from harm. Therefore, it's important that your decisions are made with this aim in mind. You must be able to evaluate different strategies, how they will be of benefit to the wider public, and take responsibility for delivering upon these. Furthermore, public service is about facing up to challenges and adversity, and overcoming these obstacles, to provide a great level of service. You must be able to engage and communicate with the public, listening to their needs and making them feel valued and appreciated.

A police constable with good public service can:

- Act with the best interests of the public in mind.

- Put the needs of the public above their own interests.

- Adapt their communication to the appropriate audience.

- Make a conscious effort to understand the needs of different members of the public.

Transparency

Transparency is a really important quality for any police constable to have. This value is closely linked with honesty. It's essentially about being someone whom others can trust and have faith in. You must be able to explain, verbally and in writing, the rationale behind your decisions. You must be genuine with everyone you are communicating with, and make a concerted attempt to build trusting and strong relationships with your colleagues. Likewise, you must be someone who is capable of accepting criticism and improving your own working practice. It's very important that you can learn from and accept your own mistakes.

A police constable with transparency can:

- Be truthful, honest and tactful with others.

- Demonstrate an honest and critical approach to their own work, accepting that there are always areas for improvement.

- Take a clear and comprehensive approach to communicating with colleagues and members of the public.

- Behave in a way that invites members of the public, and their colleagues, to trust in them and their decision making.

- Understand and maintain confidentiality.

Looking at the values, you should be able to see that these are all basic behavioural qualities that you would expect from any police constable. During the selection process, it's likely that you'll be challenged on these values – through interview questions and various exercises, so make sure you study sufficiently, learning them properly.

Core Competencies

Core competencies are a set of behavioural characteristics that all candidates are expected to exhibit. These are behavioural qualities that you will need to demonstrate on a constant basis while working as a police constable, and therefore it's vital for the police to establish that you understand said qualities, and that you've previously demonstrated them in the past.

Emotionally Aware

It's very important for police constables to be emotionally aware. Not only do you need to be emotionally aware towards the needs and feelings of others, but you also need to be emotionally aware of yourself. You must be able to control your emotions when under high amounts of pressure, and exhibit strong levels of decision making. Police work is highly stressful, and will push you to your limits. Therefore, it's vital that police employees can stay calm and collected, and manage their emotions.

Candidates must exhibit qualities such as:

- Treating others with respect and compassion.
- Acknowledging other people's opinions, values and beliefs – provided they fall within lawful boundaries.
- Asking for help when necessary.
- Recognising their own limitations, and seeking assistance in accordance with this.
- Adapting their approach to the needs of specific/different individuals.
- Promoting diversity and valuing the different qualities of individual colleagues.
- Encouraging others to reflect on their work, and supporting them to improve.
- Taking responsibility for the emotional welfare of their team members.
- Understanding the reasons behind certain organisational behaviour requirements, and playing a key role in adapting and improving these expectations when necessary.
- Using their influence in an effective and professional manner, to help resolve internal issues within the police force.

- Viewing police work through a variety of spectrums, and being able to challenge their own views and assumptions.

Taking Ownership

In order to work as a police constable, it's vital that you can take ownership and responsibility, and be accountable for your own actions. Part of this means accepting that sometimes minor mistakes will happen, but the way you deal with these is what is important. You must learn from your mistakes, and seek improvement-based feedback. Furthermore, it's critical that you can take pride in your work, and recognise your own limitations.

Candidates must exhibit qualities such as:

- Accurately identifying and then responding to problems/issues.
- Completing tasks with enthusiasm and positivity.
- Taking responsibility for their own decisions.
- Providing others with helpful and constructive feedback on their working practice.
- Promoting an internal and external culture of ownership and responsibility, so that their colleagues can also take responsibility for their own decisions.
- Play an active role in making improvements to the police force, through regular examination of police policies and procedures, to ensure that the service is operating to its maximum potential.
- Taking accountability for the decisions that other members of their team make.
- Taking personal responsibility for correcting problems that they notice within the force.
- Embracing the idea of being a role model, and using mistakes and errors as a learning process and a chance for improvement.
- Helping to instigate measures that will allow others to take responsibility in a more effective and smooth fashion.
- Looking at issues from a wider police perspective, and how they will impact the reputation of the service as a whole.
- Being someone whom others can look up to, in order to see the excellent and all-encompassing standards and values of the UK police.

Working Collaboratively

Teamwork is a fundamental part of working as a police constable; the better you can work as part of a collaborative unit, the better level of service you can provide to the public. Good police work is about building partnerships, not just with your colleagues, but with members of the public too. You must be polite and respectful with every person that you meet, and show that the police value the ideals of teamwork, collaboration and social unity.

Candidates must exhibit qualities such as:

- Working cooperatively and in harmony with colleagues and professionals from other organisations.

- Exhibiting an approachable and friendly exterior, so that others feel comfortable asking them for help or guidance.

- Showing a genuine interest and appreciation in other people, their views and opinions, in order to build comradery and rapport.

- Treating every person that they meet as an individual.

- Managing the relationship between the police service and partnership organisations, with the aim of producing long-term benefits for the general public.

- Working with partnership organisations, to create public welfare initiatives.

- Communicating effectively with everyone whom they come into contact with.

- Working amicably and professionally with members of the public, to build trust in the police service.

- Demonstrating political awareness, and an understanding of how politics can impact on the relationship between the police and their partnership agencies.

- Helping others to build relationships with external potential partnership organisations, which could be of benefit to the police and the general public.

- Setting the standard for the way in which partnership organisations interact with and work with the police service.

- Helping to create an environment that is conducive to partnership work.

Deliver, Support and Inspire

It's imperative that police constables understand the wider vision of the police service. You must use the police's values in your day-to-day work, and show a dedication to working in the best interests of the public. Your positive contribution to the police is extremely important. Police constables must show an understanding of how their behaviour impacts on the reputation of the service, and strive to make a positive contribution to this at all times. You must be focused on helping your teammates to achieve high standards, whilst maintaining your own.

Candidates must exhibit qualities such as:

- Being willing and ready to tackle challenging tasks, with the aim of improving the output of the police service.
- Demonstrating an understanding of how their work contributes to the police.
- Taking a conscientious and resilient approach to police work, always endeavouring to provide the best possible service.
- Using resources efficiently, to make a significant impact.
- Giving clear instructions to others, and helping colleagues to understand how their work impacts the wider police service.
- Breaking down potential barriers to optimal performance.
- Providing advice and support to the public and to your colleagues.
- Using resources in the most appropriate and efficient manner, to deliver a significant impact.
- Motivating others, and inspiring them to achieve success and maintain high standards.
- Constantly challenging others to maintain the vision of the police service, to the highest possible standards.
- Making conscious efforts to demonstrate to their colleagues about how specific tasks and ideas link in with the wider vision of the police.
- Helping others to understand their individual goals, comprehensibly, and how these goals fit in with the wider vision of the police.
- Monitoring changes, both internally and externally, and taking steps to guarantee positive outcomes.
- Thinking in a strategic and detailed fashion, demonstrating long-term planning and knowledge.

Analyse Critically

Working as a police constable involves large amount of critical analysis. You'll be presented with a wide variety of data, and will need to use all of this data to come to informed decisions. This is essentially what 'taking an evidence-based approach' means. It's about using the evidence available to you effectively and efficiently, to gather as many facts and hard info as possible, before using this data in the most logical way.

Candidates must exhibit qualities such as:

- Understanding the importance of critical thinking, analysis and careful consideration before making decisions.

- Assessing and analysing information in an efficient and accurate manner.

- Solving problems by using logic and sound reasoning.

- Balancing the advantages and disadvantages of actions, before taking them.

- Recognising and pointing out flaws in data or information.

- Taking information from a wide range of sources into consideration, before making decisions.

- Understanding the long-term consequences of potential actions.

- Recognising when the right time to take action is, and understanding how to limit the risks involved in said action.

- Encouraging others to make decisions in line with the police code of ethics.

- Balancing out the risks and benefits of all decisions, with consideration on the wider impact of said decisions.

- Understanding when it's appropriate to raise concerns or challenge decisions made by those in a senior position to them.

- Using their knowledge of wider policing to inform their decisions.

- Being willing to make difficult decisions, even if these decisions could result in significant change.

Innovative and Open Minded

The final competency challenges the mindset of the candidate. It's extremely important that you can take an open-minded approach to police work. Not everything is straightforward and 'by the book'. There will always be problems which require an innovative and creative solution, and it's your job to come up with this solution! Furthermore, it's essential that you can take an open mind to **new** ways of working, and understand that continuous development is a necessity for any police constable.

Candidates must exhibit qualities such as:

- Being open to new perspectives, ideas and perceptions.

- Sharing ideas and suggestions with colleagues, with the aim of improving current police practice.

- Reflecting on their own working practice and how it can be improved.

- Adapting to changing circumstances and needs.

- Using a number of different sources to gain information, using common sense, and not 'just' police criteria.

- Identifying potential barriers or problems which could present an obstacle to the way in which they and their colleagues work in the future.

- Taking a flexible approach to problems, being willing to adapt and change when necessary.

- Encouraging others to think creatively, and taking risks it is correct to do so.

- Implementing new ways of working, which can have a significant, positive change on future working practice.

- Encouraging others to review their own performance through the lens of long-term policing.

- Playing a central role in developing a positive learning culture, taking steps to promote innovation and creativity.

- Taking part in creating new initiatives, with police partnership agencies.

- Taking accountability for improvement and change within the police force.

You can find out more about the core competencies in our police core competencies blog.

The Police Constable selection process will only assess Level 1 of the Competencies Value Framework.

OVERVIEW OF THE POLICE SELECTION PROCESS

REGISTER INTEREST WITH A POLICE FORCE

↓

SUBMIT APPLICATION FORM AND UNDERTAKE ELIGIBILITY CHECKS

Note: Some Forces will implement sifting exercises at this stage, such as a behavioural styles questionnaire and situational judgement test.

↓

POLICE ONLINE ASSESSMENT PROCESS STAGE 1:

Situational Judgement Test

Note: Police forces may use their own sifting tests, in that instance, candidates will be referred straight to stage 2.

You MUST pass Stage 1 to move on to Stage 2.

↓

POLICE ONLINE ASSESSMENT PROCESS STAGE 2:

Video Interview (competency-based)

You MUST pass Stage 2 to move on to Stage 3.

↓

POLICE ONLINE ASSESSMENT PROCESS STAGE 3:

Written Exercise

Briefing/Presentation Exercise

Note: Although both exercises make up Stage 3, you will receive invitations to these exercises separately, so they do not need to be taken together.

↓

FORCE INTERVIEW (FINAL INTERVIEW)

A structured interview to establish your values and motivation for joining the police.

Note: It is up to the discretion of individual police forces if a final interview will be used. These can take place as a live video interview or may even take place in person.

Some forces will require the in-force interview to be passed before the Police Online Assessment Process stages and therefore will be conducted after the sifting tests at the start of this process.

↓

JOB FITNESS TEST, BIOMETRIC VETTING, & DRUGS TESTING

Upon successfully completing the three online assessment process stages, candidates are required to undergo a job fitness test, medical assessment, biometric vetting, pre-employment checks, non-biometric vetting, and reference check.

THE ONLINE ASSESSMENT PROCESS BREAKDOWN

The below is a breakdown of the new police officer online assessment process:

STAGE 1 - SITUATIONAL JUDGEMENT TEST

TEST LENGTH:

12 questions, approximate completion time 30 minutes to take within a maximum of 120 minutes.

The test must be completed in one session.

The test length will vary for most candidates and will be much quicker than 120 minutes to complete.

TEST OVERVIEW:

The police situational judgement test consists of 12 scenarios and questions, each containing 4 potential answers.

Once a question has been displayed on-screen, you will be required to select one answer from 4 potential answers. The answer you select should reflect what you would do in the situation described.

All of the situational judgement test questions are based on police constable scenarios.

You will not need any prior technical knowledge to complete the test, the questions are to access how you would best respond to a situation and the system will analyse if that matches with the police core competencies and values.

HOW TO TAKE THE TEST:

To take the test, you will need a computer, laptop, tablet, or smartphone with a good internet connection.

You cannot take breaks during the test; it must be completed in one sitting.

You must answer every question honestly to complete the test – you cannot skip a question.

HOW THE TEST IS ASSESSED:

This test measures your ability to make decisions that are effective and match the behaviours expected of those in the police: the competencies and values.

This test has been developed to give candidates a look into what it's like to conduct the role of a police constable, and therefore, the answers you pick will need to reflect the same values and competencies the police use.

You will know if you have passed immediately after successfully completing the test via the system.

SAMPLE QUESTION:

This question is for demonstration purposes and is not representative of the real test, instead it is intended to give you an idea of what to expect with SJT questions.

> You are sitting in the staff canteen, when three other members from your constabulary sit down at your table. As you engage in friendly discussion with them, two of the members begin to mock the other person for his religion. Although they are only joking, you can see that the individual in question has been upset by these comments.

Select the answer option that reflects how you would react in this scenario.

1. Join in, it's just a bit of banter.

2. Speak up, and inform your colleagues that they should have more respect for other religions.

3. Ask the offended colleague to speak to you in private afterwards, where you will discuss the comments.

4. Try to change the subject.

ANSWER:

'Speak up, and inform your colleagues that they should have more respect for other religions.'

This is the most efficient response, as you are clearly demonstrating to the affected individual that discrimination of any kind will not be tolerated, as well as admonishing your colleagues for their behaviour.

STAGE 2 – VIDEO INTERVIEW (COMPETENCY-BASED)

If you are successful in Stage 1, you will be sent an email inviting you to take part in Stage 2 – the competency-based video interview.

TEST LENGTH:

The test will last up to 30-minutes and consist of 5 questions.

You will have 1 minute to view the question and then 5 minutes to provide your answer.

TEST OVERVIEW:

You will be required to answer 5 competency-based interview questions using your webcam and microphone. Your answers are recorded live by the system.

You are presented with one question at a time, along with additional information in bullet points. You have 1 minute to read this information. The information will also be presented to you in the form of a pre-recorded video message by an assessor.

Candidates then get 5 minutes to answer the question.

You will not be able to rerecord your answers.

HOW TO TAKE THE TEST:

You will need a desktop computer, laptop, tablet, or smartphone with a microphone and webcam (selfie camera on a smartphone) with a good internet connection.

Adobe Flash Player will need to be installed and enabled on your device. If using a smartphone, instead of Adobe Flash Player, you will be required to download the College of Policing's "LaunchPad video interview" app.

You can refer to the information and material provided, but you are not allowed to take any notes or copies.

You cannot take breaks during the test; it must be completed in one sitting.

HOW THE TEST IS ASSESSED:

Candidates' answers to the interview questions will be assessed against the following competencies and values:

Values:

Public Service

Transparency

Integrity

Competencies:

Innovative and Open-mindedness

Taking Ownership

An assessor will review and score your recorded answers after you have completed the test. You will be sent a report on how well you matched the competencies and values being assessed against you. If you pass, you will be invited to undertake Stage 3.

SAMPLE QUESTION:

Tell me about a time when you have demonstrated your ability to be innovative.

HOW TO ANSWER:

In this question, the interviewer is clearly testing the core competency of being innovative and open minded. So, you need to think about what these competency entails, before you can respond. Remember that being innovative and open minded requires a very specific mindset. You must be someone who is creative, can problem solve, and is open to new methods of police work. So, try and demonstrate all of this in your response!

SAMPLE RESPONSE:

'Whilst working for my previous company, a business consultancy firm, I was one of the team leaders. Our team was specifically tasked with producing presentations for visiting cliental and customers, with the aim of endorsing our products and encouraging them to utilise our services.

On one occasion, my team was asked to make a presentation to a partnership agency who were considering investing a large amount of money in our company. This was a huge responsibility. Although I felt very nervous, I was confident in my ability to manage the team and produce a truly excellent presentation. I believed that, since I had given many similar presentations before, this one would be similar. I quickly got to work, assigning people individual roles and parts to present, based on their strengths. However, halfway through the planning, one of my colleagues pointed out to me that because of this company's particular viewpoint, it would be better off for us not to present in our normal way.

Initially, this threw me a little bit. I was naturally quite happy at the idea of doing something that I was comfortable with, but I quickly realised that my colleague was correct, and changed my approach. I decided to take a completely different outlook on the project, and produce something with a bit more creative flair. I knew that this was a big risk to take, but I believed that it was the right one given the circumstances, and that our normal style of presentation would not have worked. I was happy to change my way of working, with the goal of the team in mind. When I explained my new idea to the team, they all thought it was great, and praised me for my quick innovation and on-the-spot thinking.

We got to work, and ultimately produced a brilliant presentation. The partnership agency were extremely impressed, and ultimately invested even more money than we had hoped for. As a result, my managers were full of praise for both myself and my team.'

STAGE 3 – WRITTEN EXERCISE

If you are successful in Stage 2, you will be sent two separate invitations via email inviting you to take part in Stage 3 – the first of which is the written exercise.

TEST LENGTH:

The total test time will last approximately 40 minutes.

Within this time, you will need to read all of the provided supporting information and complete the exercise.

TEST OVERVIEW:

You will undertake the role of a PC (police constable) for this task, where you are required to complete an urgent written task for your direct manager.

This task is likely to focus on an issue in the community.

You will be provided four sets of information (such as, potentially, a letter or email from a member of the public) that you can use to help form your written report.

You are required to type the written exercise on your device in your web browser.

HOW TO TAKE THE TEST:

You will need a desktop computer, laptop, or tablet with a good internet connection.

At the end of the exercise, you are required to use your webcam and microphone to record your name to verify your identity.

You cannot take breaks during the test; it must be completed in one sitting.

HOW THE TEST IS ASSESSED:

Candidates' will be assessed against the following competencies and values during the written exercise:

Values:

Impartiality

Competencies:

Analyse critically

Deliver, support, & inspire

Collaborative

Taking ownership

It is essential that you only use the information provided and that you do not make any new information up in your report.

You are not allowed to use any external resources to aid your preparation – such as the core competencies and values printed out next to you.

An assessor will review and score your written exercise after you have completed this assessment and the briefing/presentation exercise.

STAGE 3 – BRIEFING/PRESENTATION EXERCISE

The second part of Stage 3 id the Briefing Exercise. This is the final part of the new police online assessment process.

TEST LENGTH:

The briefing exercise will last for a maximum of 46 minutes.

The test will be broken down into 10 minutes to prepare using the information provided and a further 36 minutes to answer the questions relating to this information.

TEST OVERVIEW:

You will undertake the role of a PC (police constable) for this task, where you are presented a scenario in which you are required to handle a series of issues.

During this exercise, you will be provided a set of questions relating to the issues from this scenario, which you must provide answers to.

You will be provided additional information and materials to aid your preparation within the first 10 minutes of the exercise.

After the preparation phase, you will have 36 minutes to present your answers broken down into the following stages:

PART 1 – Candidates are required to answer questions relating to the first part of the scenario for 12 minutes.

PART 2 – Candidates will be given further information and 4 new questions based on the second part of the scenario and given a total of 12 minutes to complete this stage.

PART 3 – Candidates will be given further information and 4 new questions based on the third part of the scenario and given a total of 12 minutes to complete this stage.

HOW TO TAKE THE TEST:

You will need a desktop computer, laptop, tablet with a good internet connection.

Candidates are recorded during the 10-minute preparation stage at the beginning of this exercise to ensure exam integrity, but you will not be assessed in these 10 minutes. Therefore, do not begin to proceed with providing your findings/answers until the next stage of this exercise.

You cannot take breaks during the test; it must be completed in one sitting.

HOW THE TEST IS ASSESSED:

Candidates' will be assessed against the following competencies and values during the written exercise:

Values:

Public service

Competencies:

Emotionally aware

Innovative & open-minded

Taking ownership

It is essential that you only use the information provided and that you do not make any new information up in your report.

An assessor will review and score your written exercise after you have completed this assessment and the briefing/presentation exercise.

Remember, you are undertaking the role of a PC, so you will be expected to answer the questions as if you are a PC with general knowledge on how the police are expected to build positive relationships and community relationships (see the competencies assessed). No technical knowledge of policing will be required.

You are not allowed to use any external resources to aid your preparation – such as the core competencies and values printed out next to you.

TOP TIPS FOR YOUR BRIEFING EXERCISE:

THINK ABOUT THE IMPLICATIONS OF YOUR DECISIONS

When you go into the briefing exercise, you will need to give clear rationale for every single decision that you've made.

CONSIDER THE STRUCTURE OF YOUR RESPONSE

It's imperative that you can properly structure your response, as this will help to make your ideas clear to the assessor. The clearer your response, the better you will score, and the more logical your ideas will come across.

COMPETENCIES & VALUES

As always, the competencies and values will play a vital role in how you are scored for this exercise. Factor the competencies into your responses – call them by name e.g. *it's important that our officers are open-minded when dealing with members of the public.* The better you can do this, the higher marks you will get.

PLAN FOR FURTHER INFORMATION AND QUESTIONS

You can't predict exactly what the assessor is going to ask you, but it's always good to have a think about what types of questions you'll be asked. This will ensure that you aren't caught off guard by anything, and can give clear and direct responses.

POSTURE MATTERS!

If you've ever performed a presentation before, then you'll be aware that how you physically present yourself can make a big difference. You need to project an air of confidence, without coming across as brash and arrogant. Remember that this exercise is just as much about convincing the police that you can make big decisions and that they should have faith in you, as it is actually producing a good report.

ANSWERING QUESTIONS

When it comes to answering questions, you'll need to do this in the correct way. It's okay to take a moment to think before speaking, as you consider what has been asked. Don't just rush into an answer without considering the question first, because if you don't answer properly then this will show that you aren't a good listener, and that you don't pay enough attention to detail – both of which are core qualities for police constables to have!

ACE THE POLICE OFFICER SELECTION PROCESS!

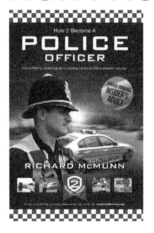

How2Become have created these FANTASTIC guides to assist you during the police officer selection process. Our products range from the initial application form, police tests, all the way up to the final interview. We also offer a 1 day course to help you prepare for each stage of the application process.

FOR MORE INFORMATION ON HOW TO BECOME A POLICE OFFICER, PLEASE CHECK OUT THE FOLLOWING:

WWW.HOW2BECOME.COM

Get Access To

FREE

Psychometric

Tests

www.MyPsychometricTests.co.uk

Printed in Great Britain
by Amazon